ENABLER?
I HARDLY KNOW HER!

HOW TO MAKE THE SALES
EXPERIENCE NOT SUCK

T. MELISSA MADIAN, P.ENG.

Enabler? I Hardly Know Her!
Copyright © 2020 by T. Melissa Madian

Tellwell Talent
www.tellwell.ca

ISBN
978-0-2288-4044-2 (Paperback)
978-0-2288-4045-9 (eBook)

DEDICATION

To all the enablers out there, especially my mom & dad.

TABLE OF CONTENTS

ACKNOWLEDGMENTS

This book would not have been possible without the fabulous experiences I have had throughout my career and my amazing clients. Shout out to my Feloquans around the world and my LinkedIn connections who provided ideas on what to cover in this book. And I would be remiss if I did not acknowledge the support of my dashing hubbie, who tolerates my shenanigans and always knows how to make me laugh.

CHAPTER ONE

WILLKOMMEN! BIENVENUE! COME ON IN!

HA – this is the Prologue! No one EVER reads the Prologues in books, so I have cleverly disguised it as the first chapter . . . and you fell for it! SUCKER!

Now that you are reading this: Hello and welcome! My name is Melissa and I'm your author. I have been in Sales for the better part of twenty-five years, the last twelve or so in an emerging field called Sales Enablement. This book will explain what Sales Enablement is, why it's important to your business, and how to successfully implement it within your organization aligned to your buyer's journey in a way that won't cost millions of dollars or lose hundreds of lives.

I've had the pleasure of building and running successful sales enablement programs for rapid-growth startups, for large corporations, and for pre-IPO software companies. I've seen how successful enablement can transform a sales organization, and how a lack of enablement can destroy one. I have tried to recreate events, locales and conversations from my memories of them. In order to maintain anonymity in some instances I may have changed some identifying characteristics and details such as physical properties, occupations and places of residence.

I'm not a fan of reading "business books" – any time a manager has asked me to read a "business book," I cringe and reach for a bottle of wine. I decided that if I'm going to write something, it's going to be something I'd enjoy reading myself. Otherwise, how could I possibly expect you to want to read it?

I could make a solid argument that what I'm going to outline in this book can be applied to other parts of an organization; say, Customer Success or Marketing. For the purposes of keeping things simple, I'll focus on Sales Enablement, with the understanding that you could extend the tenets of this book out to enabling any part of your organization. By the time you are finished reading, you should have all the pieces you need to pull together a proven and pressure-tested enablement program at your organization, regardless of your team's size or maturity. And if you still need help, I'm just a LinkedIn[1] message away.

The examples in this book are all based on my real-life experiences; I've changed names and places to protect the innocent.

Oh, and here are some definitions for terms I use throughout the book:

- Customer. This refers to a potential customer (also known as a prospect or a buyer) or a current customer. For simplicity, I'll call someone who has bought/will buy something from you a "customer" – although I may flip between using "customer" and "buyer." Author's prerogative!
- Seller. This is a gender-neutral term I use to refer to a salesperson.

---

[1]   Connect with me at: https://www.linkedin.com/in/melissamadian/. Just tell me it's because you read this book, so I know you're not a bot.

- Product. This is my generic term for any product/service/solution/software.
- Enabler. This is gender-neutral short form for someone in Sales Enablement.

So, sit back, grab a glass of your favorite beverage – or a bottle, I'm not judging – and enjoy this book!

CHAPTER TWO

WHAT THE HECK IS SALES ENABLEMENT?

My very first sales job was during the summer between my first and second year of university. My dad had a close friend who owned his own company, and he graciously took me on as his paid intern for the summer.

The company was an industrial parts supplier, selling things like chemical solvents and manufacturing parts. It didn't really matter to me – I was young and university-poor and needed the job experience. I was happy to have any job that paid during the time off from school.

On my first day, after getting through all the paperwork and getting a tour of the facility, my dad's friend/my boss showed me to my desk. He put a stack of product brochures down and said, "Read through these so you can learn about the products we sell."

I thought: Yay! I'm learning stuff! Real job stuff! Working world stuff!

Then he slapped a very large phone book on the desk next to the brochures. For those of you too young to remember what a phone book is: It's about 8 ½ by 11 inches in size, and about 4 inches deep . . . of paper, bound together, with alphabetically listed names and phone numbers. It looks like a physical manifestation of the Contacts icon on your mobile device.

He said, "This is the national manufacturers list. Call through this book and try to sell them one of our products based on the type of manufacturer they are. When you get a hot lead, record it on one of these slips of pink paper and give it to the appropriate salesperson in the office."

And then he left to do a call. That was my summer job.

How was I to get some random person whose number I found in a phone book to buy a random product that they may or may not need? Weren't my odds better if I played a lotto ticket and made the company money that way?

I sat staring at the phone book for longer than any human should stare at a phone book.

I did the only thing a just-finished-first-year university student knows how to do: I cracked open the product brochures and I started studying.

• • • • • • • •● ●• • • • • • • •

A sales organization is, outside of executives, the most expensive resource at a company. Why do organizations think that by just hiring someone with the title "salesperson" it automatically means they will be able to sell the solution? Why wouldn't time and resources be invested in training them on how to be effective in their role?

The interesting, and somewhat disturbing reality is even today a large percentage of organizations do not invest in a serious enablement curriculum for their sales reps. Companies think enablement is essentially what I experienced when I was that summer intern: learn the product by studying the available collateral and call through a database of potential leads until you reach one that is interested.

It makes about as much sense as a dog reading **Atlas Shrugged**. Not to say that a dog can't read about a dystopian society that struggles with the morality of self-interest; it just doesn't make much sense that it would. Dogs generally don't struggle with self-interest, particularly when tennis balls are lying about. Self-interest is typically a cat's purr-view.[2]

To make matters worse, two-thirds of all salespeople miss their quotas.[3] Now, in my experience, it's not uncommon for sales targets to be so unrealistically set that there is no chance for more than a

---

[2]   See what I did there? I'm so punny!

[3]   Statistic is from this sales performance infographic on the MarketingProfs blog, October 21, 2013: http://www.marketingprofs.com/chirp/2013/11909/10-things-every-sales-manager-should-know-about-sales-performance-infographic.

couple of sales folks to hit them anyway. It's a hamster wheel scenario created by today's capitalist market: companies and their board members are constantly pushing their sales forces to sell more, sell faster and set targets higher each quarter to bring in more revenue, often unsuccessfully. The result is that, on average, only a third of salespeople hit their number. In any other role in an organization that level of performance would be unacceptable! Can you imagine only 30% of a company's engineers meeting specification on a project? It would result in a lot of partially built cars, collapsing bridges and software that doesn't do anything.

The key difference is that engineers are trained in university on how to do their job effectively and safely. There aren't any university programs out there on how to be a successful salesperson. No one graduates from university with a degree in sales(wo)manship. I certainly didn't get my Engineering degree and say, "Whoohoo, I'm going to be a salesperson now!" Like many people, I fell into sales as a result of the right combination of sparkling personality and needing a, job.

Which means it's up to organizations to train their salespeople on how to sell their solution effectively and competitively, in order to give them the best chance possible to achieve the targets set for them. And it needs to be done in a way that is easy for salespeople to absorb quickly, because, to use the adage: time is money.

Who should be responsible for training a sales force? Human Resources gets a new employee settled in their new job; but those folks aren't salespeople. Marketing creates the brand messaging and all the pretty collateral out for people to browse and consume; but those folks aren't salespeople. When you take a university course in Calculus, you expect the professor to be a mathematician. When you take a job as a salesperson responsible for a substantial quota, you should expect to gain the knowledge you need from someone who understands what success in the role looks like.

And a lot of companies do just that: They have new salespeople shadow current salespeople to understand what makes them successful. Job shadowing can be highly effective in providing context for the new hire. What isn't effective is if job shadowing is the only thing a company provides new salespeople to get them up to speed. What works for one salesperson will not always work for all; and the person being shadowed may not necessarily know why something is successful. The new salesperson could pick up bad habits by strictly copying what the experienced salesperson does, which results in a salesperson clone. And if movies have taught us anything, it's that clones are bad.

If sales employees are left to fend for themselves, how can an organization be certain they are getting the most out of them in their role? If you are in a company that sells a product to a customer, there is a lot of opportunity for acquisition, growth and expansion, but quite often organizations are not structured in ways that empower their sellers to seize these opportunities.

From a new salesperson's perspective, when you are put into a situation where there are no training materials, no guidelines and only a few people have the knowledge you potentially need to be successful, you have a few options:

1. Run away screaming.
2. Sit around twiddling your thumbs until someone explains what you are supposed to be doing so you can do it.
3. Complain that this wasn't what you were expecting and that you're better than the situation.

4. Ask around to see what you should be doing, then try and copy those around you so you blend in and no one notices that you don't know what you're doing.

5. Say "screw it" and do what you believe is the right thing to do, while learning from those around you to validate if you're on the right track and adjust accordingly.

Salespeople aren't given the luxury of testing these options because they are given a very short period to get on board (typically 2-3 months) and a very large quota to hit at the end of that ramp. Your good salespeople will flutter between options 2 and 4; based on their luck, they may be marginally successful. Your great salespeople will go all in on option 5 and will either be reasonably successful, or they'll get frustrated and leave. The problem is most salespeople aren't "great." There are a lot of "good" salespeople out there, and if you don't give them every opportunity to be successful, they'll execute option 1.

This means organizations need to set an adjustable program in place that will not only train the salesperson on what they need to be successful, but when they need it and who they can look to for guidance on whether they're on the right track. This is the essence of Sales Enablement.

> **Sales Enablement is the process of arming an organization's sales force with access to the insight, tools and information they need that will ultimately increase revenue.[4]**

Now there are a couple of assumptions I'm making in my case for Sales Enablement:

---

[4]   Got this definition from the TOPO Blog: http://blog.topohq.com

1. You have a product/solution/service to sell.
2. You have someone/a team in your organization that is responsible for selling said product/solution/service.

Even if you have an established sales training program, market conditions can change rapidly. Your program needs to adapt to those changes, or you'll get caught with an ineffective sales force. It's not just about **training** sellers... it's about **enabling** them.

• • • • • • • • ●● ● ●●● ● ● • • • • •

Before Sales Enablement was a twinkle in my eye, I was a leader in an organization that was creating a space in the Software-as-a-Service (SaaS) market that no one else had penetrated, and for a few years we did well. The beautiful thing about creating a new software niche is that no one else is selling what you have, so the entire world is your oyster. The horrible thing about creating a new software niche is once you've proved it's a viable niche, competition swoops in and claims they do everything you do, but easier, better and cheaper.

Our sales team was struggling with closing opportunities because we suddenly had competition. We were used to being the only kid building castles in the sandbox. Now, other kids were coming in and building kingdoms around us.

We had the typical sales training program of learning the product and shadowing top sales reps, but nothing that could prepare our rapidly growing sales force for the competitive pummeling we were receiving. I realized someone needed to help the salesforce learn how to navigate the new selling environment in order to survive. I had to create a sales enablement program: something that would arm the sales force with the training, process and tools they needed to be successful in the moment of truth when they were confronted with a competitor, facilitated by someone who knew what it was like to be in their shoes. That realization got me to where I am now, talking about why Sales Enablement is so critical in an organization.

Enablement is more than training. It's about empowering your sales force to be successful. If you remember nothing else after reading this book: enablement to a sales team is like Alfred Pennyworth is to Batman.[5]

• • • • • • • • ● ● • • • • • • • •

Chapter Two – Final Thoughts

Is Sales Enablement right for you? Ask yourself the following:

- Do you have a sales organization that is selling something more complicated than encyclopedias?
- Is your organization growing and/or are you adding new products/services to the market?
- Are you empowering your employees with the process/ tools/training they need to be successful on an ongoing basis?

---

[5] In case you don't get this reference: https://en.wikipedia.org/wiki/Alfred_Pennyworth

CHAPTER THREE

WHAT AM I SELLING?

Although I was an entirely clueless summer intern, I did have the presence of mind to stall in creative ways while I figured out how to tackle the challenge of generating leads from a phone book. I asked my dad's friend/my boss if he could take me on some of his customer visits so I could understand how the products were used. He was very willing to share his vast knowledge of the industry,[6] so I tagged along with him during my first month on the job.

---

[6]   *Always* cater to a person's ego, it is much easier than doing stuff.

One site visit was to an automotive assembly line. The part we sold fit at the section where paint was sprayed onto the bumper of the car being assembled. I asked my dad's friend/my boss what made our part so special?

He said, "It blows at a pressure that is perfect for the application of this paint on that part."

But, why OUR part and not another supplier? Why did they choose us?

He said, "We have a great relationship, better than the other guys in the market. He trusts me, so he buys from me."

But how did you get into that relationship? Are your dads friends? Do you have compromising pictures of him?

He said, "I knew he was using an inferior part, so I called him up one day and introduced myself. I told him that by using his current part, it was costing him over x^7 in wasted paint per bumper. If he switched over to our part, he'd save that, plus more in the efficiency gain. He invited me into his office the next day and we struck a deal that has lasted for the past four years."

But, how did you KNOW?

That's when he looked me with dead seriousness in his eyes and said: "I didn't."

I must have looked like one of those Bugs Bunny cartoons when the bottom of the toon's mouth hits the floor with a loud CLANG!

---

[7]   Amount hidden to protect the innocent.

He said, "I made an educated guess based on what I know about similar manufacturing processes and the efficiency of the competitive parts. In Sales, you need to learn everything about the challenges customers have and how they can solve those challenges with what you're selling. And you must be incredibly confident that what you are selling solves that problem better than anyone else could, and that the customer would be crazy to not buy yours because of the value to them. Basically, you need to put yourself out there and be confident that you know the customer has a problem and that no one else solves the problem like you do."

I put those ideas into practice as I started calling through that phone book. I heard, "No thanks" and "Not interested" and *click!* a lot.

Do you know what it feels like to have multiple people tell you in a given day that they are not interested in anything you have to say? It's like arriving at a party, introducing yourself, and after you answer the question, "what do you do?" having every person turn their back and walk away from you. I'd like to say it builds character, but I think it more likely builds an anxiety complex that takes years of therapy to work through.

But I did manage to convince a few folks that summer to talk to one of our salespeople. And my dad's friend/my boss's words continued to resonate with me throughout my career.

• • • • • • • • ● ● ● ● ● ● • • • •

The obvious answer to "what am I selling?" is that it's the product/service/widget that a customer can purchase from your company for a negotiated price. If you were a farmer, it would be the produce you have available on your truck to sell at the local market to families, hipsters and de rigueur vegans.

It is vital that a salesperson understand what is on the produce truck. They should know every vegetable, fruit and legume in stock on that truck and the important details about said stock. They should also know what isn't on the truck, so they don't accidentally sell bananas when they're out of season.

Product teams, whether they are product management or product marketers, are typically best equipped to provide the detailed information on what it is the salesperson has available on the truck to sell. Traditionally, the product team dumps that detailed information on the seller, assuming the seller will figure out the best way to sell the stock on the truck.

The interesting nuance is that in most complex selling environments, the potential customer isn't interested in the orange that is on the truck; they're interested in all the ways that orange will help solve a problem they have; for example, scurvy.

As I learned during my summer internship, it's not enough to know the product I'm selling; I need to know everything about the challenges customers have and how they can solve those challenges with what I'm selling. I need to provide context to the customer, so they can easily understand how my product fits in their business.

What I am selling is the solution to a business challenge a customer has; the solution being something I have in stock on my truck.

One of the functions of Sales Enablement must be to translate what the product team provides on the truck – the orange – into context and language the seller can use to effectively engage the customer: dear Customer, did you know you have the symptoms of scurvy?

The fastest way for Sales Enablement to determine how to put the product into context for the seller is to go out and talk to actual customers.

Wait, you're thinking, shouldn't Sales Enablement train the sales team on the product itself first? You may think that and be right. In the same way lemmings think they are right by following other lemmings.

Without customers, a product has no context. Customers have problems that the product you are selling solves. Until a salesperson understands what those problems are, the product can't be put into context. It's like being given a screwdriver and told to enter a room. I know how to use a screwdriver; but unless I know what needs to happen in that room, giving me a screwdriver won't help anyone. It may even hurt a few people, depending on who I find in the room.

When you get the customer on the phone, there is only one question you need to ask: "Why did you buy our software?"

Regardless of how many customers you speak with and what industries they are in, the answers will inevitably boil down to two key reasons:

- We were trying to do "x" in our business and your product allowed us to do "x" in an automated, easy, cost-effective way.
- We trusted that you are the experts in solving our problem, and your expertise is why we went with you over anyone else.

In addition to speaking to customers, you may have access to customer usage data of your product. If your customer logs into your platform, or you are using a CRM (Customer Relationship Management) system to track customer activity, you have a tremendous amount of information at your fingertips that can tell you why a customer uses you. That information can articulate what it is you are selling to customers.

I have skirted around the term up until now, because it is so overused in the business world, but essentially what you are trying to uncover is the *value* your customers get from using your product. I'm not a fan of telling Enablers to articulate the value of their product because it is too ambiguous – what is valuable to one customer may not be valuable to another. Instead, if you understand why a customer uses the product, it provides the context in which you can express the value. It's the reason why a customer would buy from you and no one else; the business problem you solve in a manner that no one else satisfies. Perhaps you are the only farmer that has all-organic produce at the market, which would be highly valuable to those vegans and any obsessive new parents not wanting to pollute their little ankle biter's body with non-organic produce.

Initially when I joined that Software-as-a-Service company I mentioned in an earlier chapter, we had no solid evidence on why our customers bought from us. We had an idea, but none of our sales materials or marketing reflected it in a focused manner. After a couple of months of asking customers and analyzing customer usage data of our software, we figured out that there were a finite number of business challenges for which our customers used our software (in this case, six). Once we had that sorted, we focused all our marketing and sales content on those six business problems that our product solved, and why customers were coming to us to solve them. It's what propelled our business from a small software start-up to a really, really, ridiculously successful software company[8].

---

[8]   Yes, that's a *Zoolander* reference.

Armed with context, an Enabler has the answer to the question, "what am I selling?" In the absence of product training materials or user guides, or even a product manual, if you know why your customers are logging into your platform, you can train your sellers on what it is they are selling. Context is everything.

• • • • • • • • ● • • • • • • • • •

Once you've uncovered the common reasons why customers use your product, you need to translate them into materials that a salesperson can easily comprehend. The key with salespeople is to provide important information in a very concise manner. Think 140 characters. It's not that salespeople are stupid or lazy; they have tremendous pressure to close a lot of business in a very short period of time (typically 3-4 months), and in addition to understanding what they are selling they also need to build pipeline, negotiate deals, create contracts, etc. Salespeople need to move very quickly, and they have a limited amount of bandwidth and time in a day. Also, salespeople generally have the attention span of a cat. Enablers need to make the information easy to digest and readily available to consume.

I'm not one for sports analogies (I don't do sports) but I'll make this one exception to explain how to get your customer business use cases into the hands of your sales team. A sports team (basketball, football, etc.) has a playbook, which is a compilation of strategies the team may use during a game. The playbook contains where the players should be at any given time on the field and what they should be doing, based on the situation on the field. You can extend the concept of a playbook to a sales team: For every reason a customer uses your product, you can create a "play" for it. This "play" would articulate the business challenge for the customer (the reason why they need your product), why your solution is the best course of action for them, a list of possible questions you may get from the customer (and corresponding answers), potential objections and how to handle them and some examples of current customers who have solved the business challenge. The "play" could look something like this:[9]

By creating a "play" for each of the common reasons a customer uses your product, you then have a Sales Playbook to share with your sales team. Each "play" shouldn't be more than one page, for easy consumption, and you can always connect to additional materials within the "play."

There are a lot of sales playbook technologies out there for an Enabler to use to make distribution to a sales team easy; but before you over-engineer this, I'd suggest starting super simply and build your Playbook in something like PowerPoint or Word. One slide per

___
[9] This is a sample of a Sales Play I have created, and one of the many services I provide to clients.

"play" and post it in a central online location for your sales team to grab (ideally in their CRM, or wherever they are tracking their opportunities). That will allow you to field test the Playbook and adjust the content before you go through the time and expense of rolling out a technology.

Having a Playbook for all the common reasons why a customer uses your product is not enough to enable a sales team on what they are selling. A Playbook without practice is just a bunch of words on paper, or even worse, technology gone to waste if you've bought Playbook software. What sales teams need to do – and this will hands-down be the hardest thing you will get them to do – is PRACTICE.

My first job out of university was as a sales engineer for a process control software company. A large part of a sales engineer's role was to demonstrate the product to the customer and demonstrate it in a way that would resonate with the customer. During an industry trade show, I was running demonstrations in the booth, and I had gotten so good at the demo flow that a colleague asked how I managed to make the demo look so fluid and natural. My answer: I had done the demo so many times for customers, it just flowed naturally. When I look back, I realize now that I had practiced the demo countless times in a LIVE CUSTOMER ENVIRONMENT.[10] And yes, I got better each time I did a demo; but how many times did I botch a demo with an actual potential customer until I got the flow down?

In any other high-paying profession, it would be insane to think that someone would do what they are getting paid to do without practice. Would the cast of **Hamilton** hit the stage without hours of rehearsal? Would a basketball team enter a playoff game without practicing their plays? Would a surgeon go into a critical operation without

---

[10]   I'm yelling this, because it's so ludicrous!

having practiced on non-living items throughout their career (or living items if you're Dr. Frankenstein)?

Why is the profession of sales any different? Why do we throw product information at our sellers, or give them a detailed Playbook, and then expect them to go out there and close millions in revenue?

The next part of enabling a sales organization on what they are selling is to create an environment where the sellers can practice the various customer scenarios and receive constructive feedback so they can learn and improve. The last thing you want is to have your salespeople practicing in front of potential customers.

There are a few ways you can have your sales team practice:

1.   Design role-play scenarios to practice with your sellers. The role-play should have two parts: the customer's role and the salesperson's information. The role-play mimics what a typical customer would say in the scenario and should be challenging enough to keep the salesperson on their toes, but not so unrealistic as to humiliate the salesperson.

2.   Ask willing customers to practice with your sellers. This is a bit more difficult, as you're asking a customer to take time away from their day; but for those customers who are loyal advocates of your product, it could be part of your Customer Advocacy program.[11] In the past, I've asked customers to participate in a role play in a public sales event, like a Sales Kick Off or Quarterly Business Review meeting, so the entire sales team benefits from watching the role play and listening to the customer.

---

[11]   What is a Customer Advocacy program? That is a whole other book; feel free to ask this organization for more information: https://www.thedesiredpath. com/about.

3. Have your sellers post videos practicing their pitch on a centralized site where Enablement, other sellers and managers can view, rate and review them.[12]

Of course, a good Enabler will do some combination of the above three, just to cover all bases with the team.[13]

Early in my career, I was an account manager at a SaaS company, managing new customers just after they had purchased the platform. My role was to run the kick-off call with the customer, welcoming them to our family and making certain I understood exactly what problem they were trying to solve so I could implement the software effectively. Quite often, the sales representative who sold the platform

---

[12]   There are some good software platforms out there to facilitate this, like LevelJump: https://www.leveljump.io/.

[13]   Yeah, okay, that's another sports reference. Author's prerogative!

would be on the kick-off call, in order to introduce me and hand the customer off in a professional manner.

During one kick-off call, when we got to the topic of data sources, the customer stated that one of the reasons they had purchased our solution was because we had a two-way synchronization between their data source and our platform. I held my breath . . . because we had no such synchronization . . . and realized the salesperson had sold something that not only wasn't on the truck, it wasn't in the same country.

I calmly stated to the customer that we had no two-way synchronization. Now, this customer was from the Boston area. If you can imagine a thick New England accent yelling a variety of different profanities at you, that is what the customer's response was. He then said he wanted what the salesperson had sold him, and if we couldn't do it, we may as well end the kick-off call. And he hung up.

I calmly waited thirty seconds, and at second thirty-one I got a call from the salesperson. He said that he just assumed we did what he sold the customer, even though he had never actually logged into the platform. I burst out laughing. Then I said I'd see what I could do.

The nice thing about being at a small SaaS company filled with super-smart developers is we could look at the business scenario and if it made sense for the rest of the customer base, we could code it quickly into the product. So, we did, and the two-way data synchronization eventually became a differentiated feature of the platform. And the salesperson never logged into the product during his entire tenure with the company.

• • • • • • • • ● • • • • • • • • •

In order for your sales organization to understand what it is they are selling, it is important to get their hands on the product once they've understood the customer business scenarios. If you sell software, give them access to the software; if you sell a service, have them experience the service. The key is to put the customer's business scenarios into physical context for them: if they were the customer, how do they use the product (or service) to solve the business problem? The more comfortable a salesperson is with the product, the more confident and happier they will be in front of the customer. It puts them in the customer's shoes, and it prevents them from selling something the product doesn't do.

If you have product training materials for your customers, it's easy to make those materials part of your sales team's learning curriculum. If you do not have training materials, or if the materials are too complicated, then leverage the business use cases you've created and map them out into short "day in the life of a customer using the platform to solve this sales play" exercises. That way, a salesperson can experience what a customer does when they access the product to solve the specific problem.

• • • • • • • • • ● • • • • • • • • • •

I've talked a lot about producing materials for your sales teams on what it is they are selling. It's vital that you revisit any content and materials at least once every quarter to review and refresh. Just like the produce on the truck, you need to make certain your materials have not gone stale or rotten. No one can use a moldy orange, except for Dr. Alexander Fleming.[14]

---

[14]   Reading is fundamental, children! More on Dr. Alexander Fleming here: https://www.acs.org/content/acs/en/education/whatischemistry/landmarks/flemingpenicillin.html#alexander-fleming-penicillin.

• • • • • • ●●●● ● ●●●● • • • • • •

Chapter Three – Final Thoughts

A sales team needs to understand what it is they are selling in order to be successful. To do this, you need to:

- Know the products available on the truck for the sales team to sell.
- Understand why the customer will use that product and what value the customer will get from that product.
- Deliver this information to your sales team in a clear, concise way, such as a Playbook.
- Make the sales team practice the customer scenarios in the Playbook, so they are prepared to have the right conversation with their customer.
- Let the sales team into the product so they can understand a "day in the life" from the point of view of the customer.
- Refresh your materials so you always have the latest information on what they are selling in front of your sales team.

CHAPTER FOUR

TO WHOM AM I SELLING?

The meeting room was filled with everyone from our sales team. At the front of the room, next to a pull-down white screen with a projected PowerPoint slide deck – slightly askew so the slide wasn't totally, evenly on the screen and had an odd triangle of slide just off screen on the bland beige wall – was our head of sales.

He pointed to a menacing chart on screen. I don't know how he managed to make a chart look menacing, but it would not have surprised me if the chart suddenly blurted, "Luke, I am your father."[15]

He slapped the screen with his hand. "Sales has missed its last three quarterly targets. We will not make our number this year.

"If we do not make some adjustments quickly, no one is making any commission. And you can forget about President's Club."

Wait what? No Club?? Who doesn't love a free vacation with their significant other to a somewhat exotic, all-inclusive destination where you get to hang out with your co-workers and their significant others to make small talk around canapés while holding frozen rum beverages in your bathing suit? It's a perk to make Club! It's our right as salespeople!

"Does anyone have any suggestions on how to make our number?" he said.

Silence.

Clearing of a throat.

More silence.

Then . . .

"Why don't we share some ideas on what's working well for some of us? Maybe ask new customers why they bought from us over our competition, so we can learn from them? We can find other potential customers that look like the ones who have bought from us?" I offered.

---

[15]   *Star Wars* FTW!!!

It's possible I sprouted a second head from my shoulder, based on the way the room looked at me.

"Why don't we go through all our LinkedIn connections and start calling our connections?" offered another sales rep.

The head of sales slapped the desk. "That's a fantastic idea! We need to do more of this social selling everyone's talking about. Everyone, get your LinkedIn lists pulled and let's get cracking!"

"But..." I murmured as my colleagues streamed past me, eager to get back to their desks.

The head of sales looked at me standing there with a confused look on my face. "You got a problem with making calls?"

I like talking on the phone. I'm one of those old school salespeople who enjoy talking to people, particularly customers. What I don't enjoy is spraying contacts with a sales pitch in the hopes they might be interested in our software, desperately trying to achieve a target that is entirely unattainable. It's like fishing in a lake using cardboard as bait.

"Nope, I'll get right on it." I replied.

And I died a little inside, reflecting the beige walls around me.

When I returned to my desk, I asked my sales colleague who shared a cubicle with me a simple question: "You don't think talking to our customers is a good idea?"

We, like many software companies at that time, had adopted a fully open-concept office space, which meant multiple people sharing long desks separated by low-walls. Productivity! Collaboration!

He shook his head openly: "Why would I want to talk to our customers? Once the deal is done, it's Services' problem, and I'm onto the next deal. I've got a number to hit, and my mortgage isn't going to pay itself."

He turned back to his laptop and typed loudly away at his email. I looked around the area and all the salespeople had their backs turned to each other, facing their laptops. Some were talking into headsets, others clacking away at email like my desk mate. I may as well have been in a coffee shop, minus the smell of freshly brewed espresso and modern folk[16] playing on the speaker system.

· · · · · · · · ● ● · · · · · · · · ·

Customers have problems that the product you are selling solves and until a salesperson understands what those problems are, the product can't be put into context.

Just because a customer has a problem, does not mean everyone within the customer organization

   a.   knows they have a problem, or,
   b.   cares that they have a problem.

The key is to determine who within the organization will care enough about the problem to fix it with your solution.

By default, sales teams are told to go for the "Decision Maker:" the high-level title within the customer organization who has the budget and/or the authority to make a purchasing decision. The issue with that directive is the "Decision Maker" doesn't always

---

[16]   Yes, it's apparently a thing.

   a.   know they have a problem, or,

   b.   care that they have a problem.

Which means randomly calling a list of high-level title targets without really understanding if that "Decision Maker" is someone who could potentially know/care about the problem is equivalent to a game of roulette. Statistically you may get lucky and win but there is no real strategy; it's a game of chance.

To gain an understanding of who your target buyer is, you need to talk to your current customers to understand not only why they bought from you, but what their day-to-day looks like. Placing yourself in their shoes will help understand their motivations, fears, hopes and dreams.

Marketers often refer to this as Personas. They'll create nifty branded one-pagers that introduce you to the persona – "Meet Mary Marketer!" – and describe who Mary is, what her day-to-day looks like, and what her concerns are in her role. They are handy for Marketers, but, when a salesperson is looking for their target buyer, the majority won't look like "Mary Marketer".

As a sales or marketing organization, all you need to know is: Who at a customer cares enough about the problem to fix it. Some of those folks might be the "Decision Maker," some might look a bit like "Mary Marketer," but ALL those folks are feeling the pain of the problem and WANT to fix it.

• • • • • • • • ● • • • • • • • •

I'm in a room full of Productivity! You can tell I am because one entire wall is a whiteboard and the other walls are glass. I can use those as whiteboards if I'm being so productive I run out of whiteboard space.

And people can see into the room, so they can see how productive I'm being!

I held the blue whiteboard marker in my hand as I looked at the numbers I had scribbled on the whiteboard wall. I circled a number and pointed,

"Even if I sold every product we have to every account I'm responsible for, I still won't come close to making my quarterly target."

The head of sales said:, "Well have you found the decision maker in your key accounts? If you can find the decision maker, they'll get the budget for you."

I looked at him, then looked at the whiteboard, then looked back at him: "It wouldn't matter if I found five decision makers at each account and they had unlimited budgets – the numbers don't add up to making my target."

Behind his eyes, I could see Scrooge McDuck counting gold coins on a table, then taking a swig of brandy, getting disoriented and falling asleep in his uncomfortable wooden chair. His mouth, however, seemed to have received a jolt of espresso. He said, "If you follow the sales process, you'll make your number. Let's walk through each piece of the process for one of your accounts. First, Metrics: have you shown them the return on investment they'll receive if they buy additional licenses? Next, Economic Buyer: Do you know who controls the budget? Then, Decision Process..."

I interrupted him, which was rude, but I didn't have the patience to wait for him to go through the remainder of the ridiculous acronym that was our sales process. Not to say acronyms are ridiculous – they're remarkably useful, like NATO or UFO – it was this particular acronym that was ridiculous. Customers aren't going to fall into an acronym or a process and trying to remember the acronym itself was almost as difficult as remembering the meaning of the acronym. It would have been better if we called the process something easy to remember, like CUDDLES or MONEY; anything couldn't be as ridiculous as the actual acronym we used.

I took a deep breath and said, "I know the sales process, boss. It's not the process. It's the math. Math follows a strict process too, and it's leading me to the conclusion that no matter what I sell or how much I sell it for, I'm not going to hit my target."

You know that look someone gets when they really see you for the first time, and what they see is a knife-wielding serial killer? That's the look that crossed over his face. Then it cleared and he said, "You just need to buckle down and get it done. Are you calling enough of your contacts within the account? It's important to not get single-threaded!"

I looked at the whiteboard. One of the numbers was streaked... like the smudge of tears... Wait, did I just sigh out loud...?

I said, "Yeah boss, that's a great idea, I'll get on the phones now."

You can get on the phones, but when you have nothing to talk about and no chance to hit your number, the conversation gets a bit awkward with a customer. I couldn't think of any creative ways to sell something I didn't have to people who weren't the right buyer, so after making my requisite calls, I occupied my time doing super-productive things like surfing the internet, watching cat videos and playing Solitaire. No one noticed; my colleagues were all doing the same thing I was. Well, maybe not the cat videos.

· · · · · · · ● ● ● ● ● ● · · · ·

If a salesperson does not understand who within an organization cares about the problem they have, calling around to C-level professionals isn't going to drum up business. You need to find folks who want to make change happen within their organization; people who, regardless of their level within the organization, want to make their company better.

CEB-Gartner refers to these folks as Mobilizers;[17] people who are more interested in the improvement of processes within their company than their own professional advancement. They may not be the "Decision Maker," but they are willing to "mobilize" the internal resources to make a unifying decision. Whether you subscribe to the CEB-Gartner methodology or not is irrelevant; the idea that as a salesperson you need to talk to the person(s) who care to make change happen within their organization is absolutely valid.

And you need that person to mobilize internal resources for you, because no one person within an organization makes the purchasing decision. There isn't one Decision Maker or Persona anymore – it's a group of people at varying levels, in various roles that care about different things that are required to at least do a drive-by of what it is you are selling in order for them to give the green light. CEB-Gartner/Challenger Inc. research says it's 6.8 people[18] who are involved in a purchasing decision. And the seller won't always be given access to that group of people.

So, to whom exactly are you selling?

---

[17] The skinny on Mobilizers and consensus selling: https://www.gartner.com/smarterwithgartner/winning-challenger-sales-reps-solve-problems-and-build-consensus/.
[18] This statistic is from CEB-Gartner/Challenger Inc.'s consensus selling research: https://www.challengerinc.com/blog/more-b2b-decision-makers-want-in.

You will find your answer with your customers. Good marketers already do this to some degree when they create Personas – they model the Persona off a mosaic of current customer profiles. Just by talking to your current customers, you can create a quick template for what an ideal customer profile looks like.

Here's how to do that:

- Pull a list of your top users, the people at various customers who are using the heck out of your solution.
- Pull a list of your highest paying customers.
- Then see what overlap there is between these two lists.
- Pick up the phone and call the people on the overlap list. Ask them:

  o How they use the product: what problem does it solve for them and how does it fit into their day-to-day activity?
  o What would happen if the product were taken away from them?
  o If they were the one who decided to buy the product, what did they have to do internally to gain consensus in buying it? Who did they need to involve?

- Write all of this down into a document/spreadsheet/ presentation, along with the basic information about the companies in the overlap list (size, industry, etc.).

And BOOM! Now you have an ideal customer profile to use to train your sales team on who they should target at other companies. It doesn't need to be complicated, or over-produced, it just needs to be something simple and easy for the sales team to understand and use.

And yes, you must TRAIN your sales team. It isn't enough to produce the ideal customer profile, you need to provide the sales team with the knowledge they need to quickly figure out who that profile is within a target organization. Quick video snippets of those ideal customer profiles are one way to get the information out to the sales team; these videos put context around what the profile is interested in and it humanizes them so a sales person knows what they should listen for when talking to other similar customers.

One organization I worked with wanted to train their account managers on typical customer profiles in a creative way, in order to maximize their team's ability to quickly identify, diagnose and adapt their pitch to the profile's needs and proclivities. They first gathered all the information on customers, using the process I've outlined above. Then they determined the common customer profiles that existed within typical accounts, and gave them identities, outlining:

- The profile's key goals, motivations and interests.
- Things the profile will typically say/ask for.
- How to handle the profile and guide the profile down the path towards deciding (or qualifying them out).

I then suggested the organization get their creative team to build avatars for each profile; and here is what that looked like:[19]

---

[19] HOW CUTE ARE THESE AVATARS??? We made a whole booklet of these customer profiles.

The profile avatars and their information were provided to everyone in an infographic-style format, so it was easily available on everyone's desktops. The training consisted of group sprints where a profile's characteristics were read out loud and the group had to quickly identify the persona and explain how they would work with that customer to get them to either agree to buy or move on. Often the training would involve a role-play, to practice positioning the solution.

It was different from the typical marketing-generated personas because it identified customer profiles in the context of what they cared about instead of who they were in the organization. By leveraging current customer information, they were able to create a set of profiles that the sales team could use to quickly identify, diagnose and position to whom they should sell.

• • • • • • • • ● • • • • • • • •

Chapter Four – Final Thoughts

Telling your sales team to always go after the "Decision Maker" isn't going to cut it if that person doesn't know or care that they have a problem that your product potentially solves. The key is to find the person within the organization who is willing to make change happen and can rally their internal troops to put your product in to solve the problem they have. The easiest way to figure out to whom you are selling is to look at your current customers and profile the ones that are change agents. Then train your sales organization on how to identify and talk to those folks.

CHAPTER FIVE

HOW DO I SELL?

It's remarkable how when you're in line at a coffee shop, everyone goes out of their way to not look at each other. You're all there for the same reason: ridiculously overpriced espresso drinks. You would think the common interest would be grounds[20] for light conversation as you waited. Yet, you go out of your way to look at your phone, or stare at the floor, or silently peruse the pastry display internally debating

---

[20]   Grounds! Get it? Like coffee grounds! I am so hilarious!

whether or not to get that cake pop. I mean, it's only 120 calories! I'm probably burning that many just standing in line.

As I mentally debated with myself, a barista – that's what you call them because "coffee bartender" doesn't roll off the tongue – asked, "What can I get for you today, Miss?"

"Cappuccino, please. Non-fat milk. And a cake pop. I'm having non-fat milk, so that makes me calorie-neutral, right?"

The barista smiled politely – clearly not amused by my shtick – took my money and nodded as I moved along to make way for the next caffeine-addicted patron.

While waiting for my drink, I concluded that you can have a group of people together for the same purpose, but completely disinterested in that common purpose, focused only on their individual need.

It felt a lot like the job I was in at that time: Key Accounts Manager for a software company (read: salesperson for important customers). Everyone on the sales floor had the common goal of selling lots of software and making money; but the way we interacted with each other (didn't) was akin to the strangers in line at the coffee shop. We went out of our way to do everything EXCEPT work together to achieve the common goal.

Ah well, I thought, another day, another dollar.

• • • • • • • ● ● ● ● ● ● • • • •

So far, I've covered two of the three key elements that a sales team needs to know to sell a product successfully:

- What am I selling?
- To whom am I selling?

These two elements I bucket into the category of "knowledge" – what sellers need to know to sell effectively. Now the third element: How do I sell what it is I'm selling to the person who is interested in buying?

This category can be broken down into two areas:

1. Sales Skills & Behavior
2. Sales Process & Tools

Behavior of a sales team can dramatically impact how your organization performs. Setting the behavior of your organization ultimately comes from leadership, but Enablement is in a unique position to influence that behavior. The sales skills you enforce within an organization can directly affect how the team behaves: is it a team of individuals aiming to hit targets with little interaction with each other (like strangers in a coffee shop), or is it a team of inclusion, sharing and support?

When I worked as a Key Account Manager, our coffee shop environment caused a lot of missed quarters and team turnover. Most of the sales team, myself included, just went through the motions. Through my inaction, I allowed myself to get complacent. Through my complacency, I became isolated. Through my isolation, I became stagnant. And stagnant salespeople are not successful.

To be successful, one must be in a constant state of activity, growth and evolution. And an environment where everyone stays independent of each other doesn't foster success. Successful sales organizations are in an environment that is the exact opposite of a coffee shop.

A sales leader once asked me if I thought people were born with sales acumen, or if those skills could be taught. I strongly believe that sales skills can be taught to any person; it's the willingness of that person to adopt those skills that will make a great salesperson. And even when you have someone who appears to be a "naturally born salesperson," if they do not exhibit the right behavior that is conducive to the environment you are trying to create within your organization, that salesperson can have a negative effect on your sales team.

I remember one salesperson who was naturally charismatic: he loved to open doors to potential buyers and he loved the thrill of the close. He was highly successful and made his number every quarter. And then we terminated his employment. Not because he wasn't successful. It was his behavior. He was cancerous to the rest of the sales organization. He'd step on his teammates to get ahead in his numbers, he wouldn't share information with his counterparts, and he was terrible at following sales process, which made it impossible for the business to predict revenue each quarter. The leaders at the organization decided they would rather have a sales team that was inclusive and supportive, that leveraged a set of positive sales skills and behaviors to close business, than have an organization full of lone cowboys all randomly shooting at various targets. What we lost by his departure, we gained by having a more cohesive, consistent, revenue-generating team of sales professionals.

When you think of the term "salesperson," what does that evoke? Perhaps you're conjuring up an image of Blake from *Glengarry Glen Ross* (if you're around my age) or Jordan Belfort from *The Wolf of Wall Street*. Charming, personable, sassy . . . or sleazy, stubborn, materialistic? Salespeople have become a trope of themselves, due largely to how the fictional world has portrayed them. It's a trope that can be overcome by focusing your sales organization on the sales skills and behaviors that you want them to exhibit when they are interacting with a customer.

Determining the key sales skills and behaviors for your sales team can be as simple as creating a 2 x 2 grid, or as complex as creating a set of seller competencies for your various sales roles. I personally like to keep my enabling simple and scalable, so here is an example of a sales skills grid that I recommend to clients:

Hits quota Doesn't use available processes & tools Not a team player Is a jerk	Hits quota Uses available processes & tools Team player/Mentor Displays enthusiasm
Doesn't hit quota Doesn't use available processes & tools Not a team player	Doesn't hit quota Uses available processes & tools Team player Displays enthusiasm

As an organization, you can manage your people against the above grid as follows.

Top-Right Quadrant – Your Superstars

Ideally an organization wants its sellers in the top-right quadrant of the grid: someone who hits their quota and is also exhibiting the skills and behaviors of a seller who fits into the team culture. Perhaps someone who is willing and ready to lead their peers one day!

Bottom-Right Quadrant – Your Atta-Boys/Girls

If a seller is in the bottom-right quadrant, it means they fit the sales culture, but need some training/coaching on hitting their quota. Perhaps they don't have the sales process down, or maybe they just need practice before they get in front of a customer.

Bottom-Left Quadrant – Your Newbies or Nobies

If a seller is in the bottom-left quadrant, it means they are new to the sales organization and are still learning, or they are struggling to fit into the sales process and/or culture. Give them a chance or encourage them to find their happiness elsewhere.

Top-Left Quadrant – Your Jerks

If a seller is in the top-left quadrant, it presents the organization with an interesting challenge. If that seller isn't a team player, and is not willing to be coached into being a team player, yet that seller crushes quota, do you keep that seller? As an organization you need to decide if culture is more important than hitting quota. SPOILER ALERT: Culture is always more important in the long run.

With your sales skills and behaviors grid this simple, it's easy for the sales manager to monitor and coach on a regular basis. At a minimum, sales managers should check in with each of their sellers on a quarterly basis, using this grid as their guide.

If simple isn't your thing, or if your Human Resources department demands more of a stringent guideline on sales skills, then sales competency grids may be the appropriate way to go. I don't have a problem with competencies as a philosophy, I have a problem with their practical application. If you have a long list of competencies, they can become unwieldy and difficult to monitor and manage. Sales managers, like salespeople, do not have a lot of time to spend coaching against a list of competencies; which means it falls to a low, and probably once-a-year priority.

Whether you are into simple sales skills grids or sales competencies, you need to put something into place for managers to set expectations and to use to coach their people towards excellence. The behaviors of your sales people greatly impact the performance of the organization as a whole.

• • • • • • • • • • ⬤ • • • • • • • • • • •

If you have ever baked a pie, you know that you must have a set of defined ingredients and steps executed in a particular order to get the outcome of a successfully baked pie.

Let's look at the ingredients for an apple pie:

- Apples
- Brown sugar
- Eggs
- Flour
- White sugar
- Salt
- Cinnamon
- Vanilla
- Butter
- Lemon

If you toss all those ingredients together, you will not end up with a pie. You will end up with a raw apple slurry that no one wants to eat.

Now let's look at the instructions for baking an apple pie:

- Bake the dough.
- Make the apple filling.
- Make the dough.
- Fill the cooked pie with apple filling.
- Heat the oven to 325°F[21]

---

[21]   Or 163°C for my fellow Canucks.

For those bakers out there, you know these instructions are not getting you to a delicious apple pie. Instructions must be more detailed, in the correct order, and involving the ingredients so you know when to apply an ingredient at the correct step in the pie-making process in order to achieve maximum pie deliciousness.

The sales process is like baking a pie; instead of ingredients you have sales content and instead of instructions you have sales stages and activities. When you are detailed about each sales stage, the activities that must be done at each stage and the content that is available to the seller at each stage, you have a recipe for a successfully closed opportunity.

First, your sales stages. These are the measured steps in the journey of a prospective customer going from someone who has no idea who you are to purchasing your product. A lot of organizations create the sales stages from their perspective for forecasting purposes:

- Rep Engaged
- Discovery
- Solution Presentation
- Proposal
- Negotiation
- Contract Signature

This is only half of the view – it's critical you also consider the customer's perspective along the buying journey. After all, if your buyer isn't at the same stage as your seller, you've got two different pies being baked. Here is a reimagining of the above sales stages, but from the buyer's perspective:[22]

---

[22] SiriusDecisions (now Forrester) is great for this research: https://go.forrester.com/research/siriusdecisions/

- Awareness
- Interest/Consideration
- Evaluation
- Decision
- Commitment
- Purchase

If you really want to take your sales stages to the next level, you will factor in what the buyer is thinking at each of the above stages. This allows your sellers to get into the head of the buyer, so they can guide the customer on their buying journey. Here is an example of the above stages, adding in what the buyer is thinking at that stage:

- Awareness = Wait, do I even have a problem that needs solving?
- Interest/Consideration = Is my problem that bad or can I manage with what I've currently got?
- Evaluation = I guess I should look around at other vendors like you if I'm going to go through with this.
- Decision = Ugh, do I really need to do this now?
- Commitment = No really, should I spend any money on this at all?
- Purchase = Oh boy, now what have I done???

Now that you have your sales stages defined, from both the seller and buyer perspective, you can determine the key activities the seller should do within each stage in order to help the customer buy from you and to keep them on track. Your messaging should take into consideration what the customer is doing and thinking, in order to equip your seller with buyer motivation at that stage. Finally, map all the content you have within your organization to each stage, to help the seller along. These are your baking tools, like spatulas, pie pans and stand mixers.

When you have the full recipe for your sales process defined and mapped, you then apply it to your CRM system, so everyone is held accountable to the same standard, allowing your business to run its forecasts effectively and predictably.

And now you have a completed recipe for a seller to use to cook their prospective buyer into a delicious customer pie![23]

• • • • • • • • • ● • • • • • • • • •

Once you have your sales process recipe established and documented, you can IMPROVISE. The best recipes have its foundation in process but have a little touch of *air kiss* that makes them amazing.

I am a strong believer that every sales professional should have improvisational skills; after all, no process is absolute or can prepare you for what a potential customer may demand. Improv teaches you three key things that are critical in any selling situation:

Respect the Ensemble

In improv, you respect the ensemble: you are a group of equally talented individuals, and as a team you need to present a scene to the audience and not step on another team member's toes in order to steal the spotlight. As sales professionals in this highly collaborative age, respecting the ensemble is critical to a sales team's success. The more you collaborate and share with your peers, the more likely sales individuals will achieve target – which is good for everyone!

---

[23]   This is a metaphor, and not an endorsement for cannibalism.

Resilience is Key

How you respond to the one heckler in the audience, or a joke bombing, can define who you are as a professional. Throughout my career I've had to deal with failure as well as success. I've learned to be a duck and let the water roll off my back. When I first began the process of starting up a Sales Enablement Services business, I was a little freaked out and there were so many things that could have gone horribly wrong. Resilience and belief that you can succeed in the face of seemingly insurmountable odds is key. Especially when it means not everyone will agree with you, which leads me to . . .

Be Authentic

So many companies say they are authentic. So. Many. Companies. Authenticity isn't about asking people "What could I do to make you like me more?" and then repeating that back. It's about being true to yourself and accepting that not everyone will have the same perspective as you. Or even like you! And that's okay. As a sales professional, if you don't believe in the product/service you are selling, the customer will sense that and not want to work with you. Why should they buy from you, if you don't believe in it yourself?

Improvisational skills can make a sales organization stronger together, resilient to changes and effective by believing in themselves. It allows them to take the sales process that has been created and improvise from it to make the customer's experience unique and delightful.

• • • • • • • • ● ● • • • • • • • •

I've spent a lot of time on sales process in the context of the customer's journey, as it is so critical to how a salesperson sells. It is, however, only one part of the equation; the other is the sales tools used to facilitate the buying process.

The biggest mistake I see organizations make is to throw sales tools at the sales team in order to make them more effective. The issue is that tools don't solve that problem –process improvement does.

Let's look at this like an Engineer.[24] Efficiency is measured by how much work or energy is conserved in a process. Efficiency is calculated as the energy output, divided by the energy input, and expressed as a percentage. The closer you are to 100%, the more efficient your process.

Say I'm trying to hang a picture on a wall. I put 20 J[25] of energy in to one strike of my hammer on the head of a nail. The energy transferred to driving the nail into the wall is 8.0 J. The efficiency of my hammering is therefore 40%. Vibrations and heating of the nail are two possible reasons for the energy loss experienced. Knowing that, I can adjust the tool I use to be more efficient or adjust how I hit the nail to use less energy. What won't help is adding a screwdriver to this scenario.

Extracting this theory to the concept of sales efficiency: If you are going to add sales tools into your process, you need to make certain that the tools either lower how much effort the sales person needs to put into the selling process or raises how much energy gets output, so you have an overall efficiency as close to 100% as possible.

If you are a sales tool vendor, the easiest target to sell into is any salesperson at that company you're trying to reach. Sales managers in particular are the biggest pushovers when it comes to taking phone calls and watching demos from vendors – any chance to put something in to look like a hero to their sales team is a no brainer!

---

[24] Which I am! Mechanical Engineer, from the University of Toronto, class of ~~REDACTED~~ because I am not exposing my age.

[25] Joules, which is the unit of measure for energy.

This is where Sales Enablement can provide a buffer, to slow down any potential flood of tools coming into the sales organization that claim to be a productivity save, but in reality will just add time and energy to a sales person's daily activities, thus lowering their efficiency.

I realized early on in my enablement career that the sales team is like any other customer you are trying to reach: you need to hit them with the right message, at the right time, in the right channel. Enabling a sales team is like a dance where delivering the right content via the right tool requires rhythm and timing. Get it right, and you are a contender for *World of Dance*; get it wrong, and you're on *The Gong Show*.[26]

I have managed to tackle this challenge using a two-step process for getting Sales operationally ready to hit the dance floor, in full sequins and jazz hands.

Step 1 – Figure out what tools the reps are currently using.

There are so many sales tools out there right now. So. Many. Tools. I worked with one organization that had a sales team of about 80 people worldwide and every regional team was using a different set of sales technologies to help them with their day-to-day operations. Some were integrated into their salesforce automation platform, and some were not. Hello, where's the efficiency here?

Sales tools should be used like any other tool: for the purposes of making something you do more efficient/effective. The challenge for most sales organizations and Enablers is that there is so much sales technology out there doing a variety of niche things to help sales teams, it's hard to make sense of what to choose.

---

[26]   Both excellent shows.

It's like using twenty-eight different spatulas, mixers and pans to bake one pie in the middle of your backyard. I mean, just look at all these options![27]

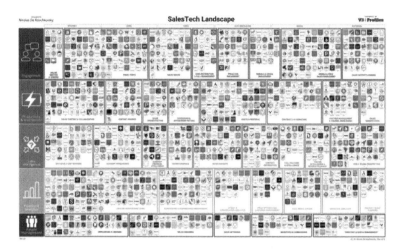

There are three key things to keep in mind when doing an inventory of your sales tools:

1. What problem(s) is (are) this tool solving for the sales organization?
2. Is the tool completely integrated into my CRM?
3. Do I already have a tool doing something similar that can be replaced by this new tool?

By doing a simple tool and content inventory within your organization, you can determine what to keep, what to toss and what you need to refresh. It's like doing a closet cleaning, without the tears and self-loathing.

Step 2 – Get your content into one or more of the above tools

---

[27] 2019 chart from SalesHacker: https://www.saleshacker.com/salestech -landscape-2019/.

There are a lot of departments within an organization that produce fantastic materials for sales to use with customers: Marketing, Product Marketing, Sales Enablement and even other sellers! The challenge is this content often gets posted in random places and Sales has no idea where to go to get it, or even when the content should be used.

Inventory your content and use one of the tools from your inventory (see Step 1) to organize the content in a way that makes sense for your sales team to consume. If you have your sales process mapped, then maybe your content is relevant by sales stage. Or maybe your content is persona or vertically focused, so it should pop up when a sales rep is working a specific vertical or with a specific persona at a customer. Having this content integrated into the CRM allows sales reps to have one place to go to access all the information they need, at the right time, in order to shine when they dance with their customer.

· · · · · · · · · ● · · · · · · · · · ·

Chapter Five – Final Thoughts

- Keeping your skills set small and scalable makes it easy for sales managers to measure and monitor the performance and behavior of the sales team.

- When you map out your sales process, do it from the customer's perspective. That way you are guaranteed a process that brings the customer with you on the buying journey and doesn't leave them behind, resulting in stalled deals.

- So. Many. Sales tools. Pick a couple that reduce repetitive administrative tasks and maximize your sellers' time, increasing their efficiency. And absolutely, positively, 100% make certain any sales tools are fully integrated into your CRM system.

CHAPTER SIX

WHOM DO I SERVE?

Sales teams are constantly being barraged with directives from management. Challenge a prospective customer! Provide them with unique insight! Break status quo! Make your number! If you don't eat your meat, you can't have any pudding![28] If you are a sales rep trying to hit your number so you can put food on the table, it's a challenge to put these directives into practice without any guidance or training.

---

[28] For you Pink Floyd fans: https://www.youtube.com/watch?v=n5diMImYIlA.

The responsibility for providing a unique customer experience lies with BOTH Sales & Marketing. From the moment a prospective customer engages with your brand, through to sale and post-sale, the customer's experience should be consistent and considered.

As a marketer, you should be out in the field with your sales professionals, hearing the language of the customer, understanding the customer's interests and struggles so you can take that back and create materials that will support your sales teams in their quest to provide unique insight. It is the best way for everyone to be on the same page when it comes to providing value and a unique experience to the customer.

As a sales professional, you are the subject matter expert on your accounts. You know what has worked well for similar customers and how your solutions can help them grow their business. You have the power to challenge your customer's way of thinking, because you've seen it all before with your other customers. It's your job to feed that information back into Enablement and/or Marketing so they can craft the messaging and materials to support that insight.

Which begs the question: **Where should Sales Enablement reside in your organization?**

If you are in Marketing, your definition of Sales Enablement may sound something like the ability to provide Sales with the content they need, when they need it. Sales Enablement software platforms have generated a lot of buzz around this definition of Sales Enablement, understandably so since they are trying to create a market in which to sell things; but content is only a small portion of what Sales Enablement is all about.

If you are in Sales, perhaps your definition of Sales Enablement is training. Train the sales team, run new hire boot camps,[29] make sure they are consuming their learning packages and get their managers involved if they are not taking their training. Except learning materials are also a small portion of what Sales Enablement is all about.

Which means I need to make a modification to the earlier definition of Sales Enablement:

Sales Enablement is about providing the revenue-generating functions of an organization with the process, tools and training they need to create, keep and develop customers, with the intent of building customers for life.[30]

Enablement along the *entire* customer lifecycle is critical to the longevity of an organization.

The content and training in Sales Enablement should encompass three major categories:

1. Knowledge – What is "on the truck" for me to sell as a salesperson; what and to whom I'm selling.[31]
2. Skills – The skills I need to be successful as a salesperson at this company.[32]

---

[29] The term "boot camp" is popular when referring to new hire training. As if Sales is even remotely close to the intensity of training for the military. Spoiler alert: It is not. I prefer "onboarding" – more realistic, less extreme. More about onboarding later!

[30] This is MY definition of Sales Enablement, and it's totally the best one.

[31] See Chapters Three and Four.

[32] See Chapter Five.

3. Behaviours – The process by which I drive my opportunities to close, and the tools I use to facilitate that process (how I sell).[33]

These three categories cross multiple departments. That is where a Sales Enablement function can really provide value; by being that connective tissue between departments to help develop, consolidate and deliver the materials, training and processes that Sales needs to be successful.

Imagine your Sales team are all in a fabulous night club with your prospects and customers. In front of that club is the Sales Enablement function, acting as the bouncers. Any department trying to get into the club to give something to Sales – content, training, knowledge, tools, a new process – must go through the Sales Enablement bouncer who determines whether the information is something Sales can use at that moment in the club. If not, the department needs to get in line behind everyone else trying to get in. Or perhaps the information is valuable, but not well presented – sir, you can't wear those sandals in this club! – so the department needs to modify the information in a way that is consumable for Sales before they can enter the club.[34]

Which means that Sales Enablement should sit under the Sales department, as the gatekeeper to all things for Sales. Or under the Chief Revenue Officer or a similar role who handles all revenue-responsible functions in your organization. The organization should look something like this.

---

[33] See Chapter Five.
[34] In other words: Sales...but make it FASHION!

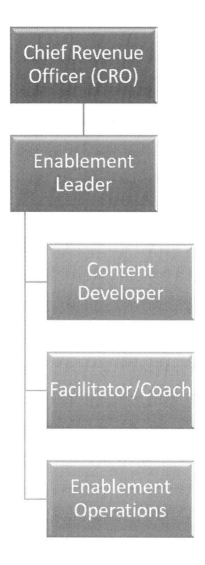

Having the function sit under Marketing is not a bad thing; it's just not the most effective place for Sales Enablement to live and thrive. Remember that the customer for Sales Enablement is the Sales team. If the function sits in Sales, then Enablement is viewed as an extension of the Sales team – Enablement has direct access to what Sales needs, and why they need it, and can translate that back to the departments that provide content, training or support. Tie Enablement's compensation to the performance of the Sales organization, so their mandate is clear.

Plus, there is a credibility play here. Sorry Marketing, but a Sales Enablement department's street cred goes WAY up if they sit under Sales. If Enablement sits in Marketing, the function will only ever be viewed as a Marketing resource responsible for content and product information, and not related to revenue.

The key thing to determine in your organization is to what metric are you holding your Sales Enablement function accountable? If the answer is external content consumption and distribution, with a splash of training, then you probably have a Marketing-centric view of Enablement. Instead, consider holding Sales Enablement accountable to metrics that matter in Sales – effects on pipeline growth, deal velocity, deal size – these metrics force a Sales-centric view of Enablement, designed to encourage the creation, retention and growth of customers.

• • • • • • • • ● • • • • • • • • •

I often get asked when an organization should consider putting in an Enablement function. And my answer is: It depends.[35] If you are a small organization (5-100 salespeople), have a good sales process and a solid sales leadership team that is willing to dedicate a portion of their time to enabling their people, then you probably don't need a full-time Enablement team in place.[36] If you are a huge, worldwide organization with a portfolio of products and services with tens of thousands of salespeople, you probably need an Enablement organization.

---

[35]   Typical consultant response!

[36]   And can instead do it with the help of plucky consultants like me! And by "like me" I mean "me."

In either case, the foundation for an Enablement function to be successful is the support of the executive and manager layers. Without their backing, the function will never be viewed as a strategic within the organization. More on this later in this book.

My suggestion to any organization is to do an assessment of where your organization is at regarding the main tenets of Enablement (Chapters Two–Five). Assess yourself on a scale of "we're in good shape" to "oh, my cat, we have nothing in place and have random acts of enablement happening everywhere" to determine if you need a full-time Enablement person.

And it's really okay if you don't need a full sales enablement function! To be fair, most of my business is built on organizations who DON'T have the function and need guidance.[37] What I have seen work well for smaller organizations is to put a solid process in place, then divide the Enablement load amongst sales enablement-y[38] functions, like product marketing or sales leadership.

• • • • • • • • ● ● ● ● ● ● • • • • •

Chapter Six – Final Thoughts

Sales Enablement can't do the job without strong relationships with Sales, Sales leadership, Marketing, Product Marketing, and Customer Success . . . essentially all the roles who interact with the customer. It's important for Sales Enablement to be the bouncer to the fabulous Sales night club, and play nice with other teams to break down siloes with empathy, letting the right information into the club at the right time, while still being sympathetic to the load the club can handle at any given time.

---

[37]   Let's talk: melissa@melissamadian.com

[38]   It's a word now!

CHAPTER SEVEN

WHERE DO I BEGIN???

I sit with many new sales enablement professionals to coach them on how to structure the function within the organization. What is common across these new sales enablers is an uncontrollable panic: Why would a tenured sales organization listen to them?

I can sympathize. If you've never done Enablement before, or if you've never sold before, your street cred is at an all-time low with the sales team. So, there is one very simple way to get a sales organization to accede to an Enabler's plan: Get. Them. Involved.

Ask them where they believe they are struggling and where they could use some training/coaching. Have them contribute into their own enablement plan!

The quickest way to get your sales team involved is to send out a sales skills self-assessment.[39] Ask the reps to assess themselves on a scale of 1 (*I really need help!*) to 5 (*I'm an expert!*). Design the self-assessment around the standard categories needed within a sales organization:

- **Knowledge.** The products and/or services a salesperson can sell; i.e., what is "on the truck."
- **Sales Skills.** Skill areas that are a challenge for the sales reps; i.e., negotiating, presentation skills, tonality, storytelling, etc.
- **Tools/Behaviors.** Ensuring that the teams are leveraging the available tools, process and resources in the right way to close business and create an exceptional customer experience that builds customers for life.

Within these categories, you can break the self-assessment down into specific questions around product, industry, sales process, sales tools and sales skills. For example:

- I understand my company's value and differentiation in the industry.
- I understand product value and differentiation for the ideal customer profile.
- I can create and effectively deliver an elevator pitch.

---

[39] Or "survey" if "assessment" is too scary a word for your sales team.

- I understand each sales stage objective and tasks / resources/timing required provide objective evidence to move to next stage.
- I demonstrate the ability to leverage tools in creation and preparation for calls.

Once you have the questions for the self-assessment ready, you must review it with the sales leaders. This will allow your management to contribute to, and more importantly reinforce, the assessment with their teams.

When you launch the assessment to the sales team, be extremely clear on its purpose: To identify the strengths/weaknesses within the team and determine the key skills to focus on in Enablement based on where they feel they need the most help. In other words, if you don't contribute, don't complain about the enablement plan you get later, Sales Team.

One thing to note: Don't overwork the self-assessment. Give the team roughly three or four days to complete it, then close it out. It should take less than ten minutes to fill out and should be the gut-reaction responses of the team. Once the self-assessment is closed, you can determine the key skills to focus on and design your training and enablement around those key areas. And voila, you've got an ongoing skills development plan for the next three to six months. I would recommend revisiting the assessment every six months or so, just to keep the data from the field fresh.[40]

* * * * * * * * * ● ● ● ● ● ● ● * * * *

---

[40] Since I've done these multiple times, I have assessment templates that you can purchase. All part of the wonderful services I provide!

The good news is most organizations will do anything and everything for their sales team. The bad news is most organizations will do anything and everything for their sales team . . . resulting in a lot of random acts of Sales Enablement.

As a new Sales Enablement professional, it may be tough to enter an organization where everyone has had the luxury of directly providing Sales with the information that they think is important. As soon as you arrive, you need to become the bouncer I mentioned in the previous chapter, and throttle those requests . . . while also organizing what already exists.

Whenever I go into any new client, the first thing I do is a thorough assessment of the organization.[41] This allows me to get a sense of their current state of Enablement, so I can set a baseline for all my recommendations.

My assessments follow the same guidelines, regardless of the size or structure of the organization:

- Inventory all sales tools and how they are being used/not used.
- Inventory all content and how it's being used/not used.
- Inventory any sales processes, or lack of processes, and how the processes are delivered and reinforced.
- Inventory any sales training (past or future) and the feedback from the training.
- Interview the sales leadership and selected salespeople. Ask them what's working, what could be improved, and what their day-to-day looks like.
- Interview Customer Success, Marketing, Sales Operations and anyone else who interfaces with Sales and/or interfaces

---

[41] Yet another service I provide!

with customers. Ask them what the relationship with Sales is like, what's working, what could be improved and how everyone serves the customer.

Once I have a complete view of the current state of the sales organization, I can make a series of recommendations on how to keep or improve upon what already exists. Then I can set a project plan with timelines for the organization to execute the recommendations.

As a new Sales Enablement professional, completing this kind of assessment will give you a clear plan of attack for your organization, thereby avoiding any random acts of Enablement that you may be asked to do. The plan gives you the authority to question incoming requests that deviate from the plan and prioritize your Enablement accordingly.

· · · · · · · · · ● · · · · · · · · · ·

Perhaps you are ready to hire for a Sales Enablement role. Quite often, I get asked if I "know anyone" who is looking for a role in Sales Enablement. The great news is that Sales Enablement is not only a thing now, it's a hugely popular thing. The bad news is there are not enough people out there with "Sales Enablement" in their title to make finding the right candidate easy for an organization.

Although I have a rather extensive network, I am by no means a recruiter. What I can do is detail on these pages what I have seen make for an excellent Sales Enablement professional, and where to potentially find them.

Your Sales Enablement professionals (those who have "Sales Enablement" in their title or job description) are typically one of two types:

1. Started in a sales role, fell into Enablement.[42]
2. Started in a Learning & Development (L&D) role, moved into Enablement.

My bias is towards type 1, because these folks understand what it means to be a salesperson and what is needed for a salesperson to be successful.[43] They've lived the role and bring that credibility to the Enablement function. That is not to say your L&D folks aren't great Enablement professionals, they just have a different point of view that tends to be more focused on training. There are pros and cons to both – choose what is most applicable to your organization.

It is possible you have looked and haven't found folks with Enablement in their background. I've had tremendous luck sourcing Enablement candidates from other parts of the organization who are doing enablement-like activities, but just don't have it in their title or job description. Look for your potential Enablers in your Sales Development team, your Product or Field Marketing teams, or even your HR team.

The type of candidate you are looking for is someone who understands what the selling process is, what a salesperson needs to be successful at each stage of the process, and how a customer gets value from your product/service. The candidate should also have a genuine passion for helping Sales, whether it be through facilitation, content creation or coaching. They also can't be afraid to say NO when Sales is issuing unreasonable demands.[44]

Once you've found your candidate, ask them three key questions:

---

[42] Me.

[43] I'm naturally biased towards people like me. Who isn't biased towards me – I'm fabulous!

[44] As Sales is wont to do.

1. What Enablement programs have you built?
2. How did these programs directly impact revenue generated?
3. How did these programs change rep efficiency/productivity?

If your candidate cannot answer these questions, you have someone who may be great at sales training, but not necessarily sales ENABLEMENT. In my experience, if you can't tie the effects of your Enablement to revenue generated or productivity gained, then you're just a training function that can be easily cut from the organization.

Chapter Seven – Final Thoughts

Getting started in Enablement may seem daunting, as there are so many things you could tackle and they all seem to have a high priority. If you're not sure of what to do first, try:

- Doing an inventory of all your sales tools and how they are being used/not used.
- Doing an inventory of all your sales content and how it's being used/not used.
- Do a skills assessment for the sales team.

In other words, start with your current state then build from there, prioritizing accordingly.

Once you are ready to hire for Sales Enablement, do not restrict yourself to just looking for Enablement professionals; often, your best Enablers are hiding in other roles within your organization.

Finally, make sure that whatever Enablement programs you run can be tied to revenue generation or sales productivity gain. This allows you to set the Enablement function up for success!

DO I REALLY NEED A BOOT CAMP?

Onboarding is one of those areas that organizations think they have on lock, but in reality is "just okay."

Your sales onboarding process probably consists of shadowing other sales reps, reading a bunch of documents and watching product training videos. Maybe a one-week boot camp where a revolving door of subject matter experts spew slide after slide of information at them.

Some years ago, I was tasked with an interesting challenge: The organization was going to hire five hundred new college graduates and wanted a twelve-week onsite training program[45] to onboard them into the inside sales function.

Why twelve weeks? Well, the executives making the request had experienced a similar onsite training program when they started out in their careers and felt that it greatly contributed to their success. They wanted these new sales hires to have the same training experience; making the new hires feel like they were part of an amazing sales culture and setting them up for success in the team.

There were so many flaws in this logic. First off, the world had changed significantly since these executives were college graduates. How folks learn and collaborate today is different than back then. Secondly, technology had changed; which meant in-person facilitated training wasn't the only option available. And finally, having to manage five hundred college graduates in a confined space for twelve weeks sounded less a career opportunity for me and more like a form of slow torture.

At the time, however, I enjoyed my paychecks, so instead of raising these points, I sucked it up and designed an on-site training program to satisfy the request of the executives. The program still runs to this day, modified from the original version. I still keep in touch with a couple of the hires that went through the first iteration of the program; funnily enough, they are not at that organization anymore.[46]

---

[45]   Ugh, yes, in other words a "bootcamp".
[46]   But they did enjoy the experience, because even though I disagreed with the idea, I still crushed it at my job.

· · · · · · ●●● ● ●●● ● · · · ·

Why do I have such a hate-on for boot camps? Isn't it a good idea to bring the new hires in to meet everyone and experience the organization's culture?

To be clear: My issue isn't with bringing everyone together to build camaraderie and culture. My issue is the assumption that after one week's worth[47] of an on-site training boot camp, the salesperson should know everything they need to know. And when they go back to their desks and they don't close deals, the organization blames the rep on not doing their job. In reality, the organization never enabled them to do their job effectively.

If you have never played a piano, would you expect to learn sheet music in a room for one week, then sit down and perfectly play a sonata? Why would you expect a sales rep to be any different?

To empower the sales rep to sell effectively, an organization needs to arm them with:

- What problem am I solving with my solution?
- Who cares about this problem?
- How do I convey the pain of this problem effectively, so the person I'm speaking with understands that they need to care deeply and immediately enough to solve the problem?

To onboard a new sales rep effectively with the above information, an organization should execute the following onboarding sprints:

- LEARN: Online videos, scripts, documents, anything you need them to consume to understand the key points

---

[47]   Or twelve weeks' worth.

mentioned above. This is the equivalent of learning your scales and sheet music when learning how to play the piano.

- PRACTICE: Just like you would sit at the piano and practice your scales and songs, your reps need to practice the messaging. Have them practice with each other, practice with a manager or peer coach, practice with subject matter experts.

- DO: Your piano teacher typically sits next to you as you play the sheet music and will comment on and coach your performance. The rep's manager or peer coach should do the same as a rep does dry-runs of calls, emails and voicemails. Leverage technology to have reps post videos/recordings of themselves doing a pitch, or call, or presentation, so others at the organization can comment or rate their pitch.

Every new topic, message or script should follow the above sprint cycle, so the rep has an opportunity to truly internalize the message. That way, when they "step onstage" in front of a customer, they are ready to play some great music.

And give the information to the rep when they need to know it, not in one firehose spray of information. For example, they don't need to know how to negotiate your legal agreements until well into their second month on the job; so why have them meet with the legal team during a one-week boot camp? Your onboarding process should provide your reps with the information they need, when they need to know it and not before. In their first week, they are just trying to figure out the simple things like who everyone is and how their role fits in the organization. In the second week, it's about how to be a good salesperson at the organization. In their third week, it's about learning what your products/services do for customers and in their fourth week (and beyond) they need to know how to run their franchise as a sales rep. In summary:

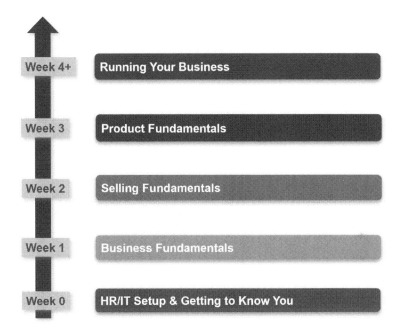

Using these thematic guidelines for each week, here is an example of what an onboarding program could look like for a new sales rep:[48]

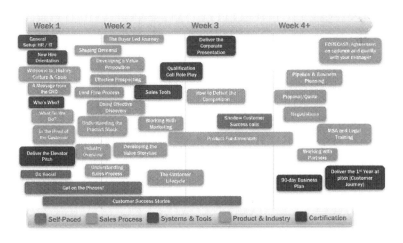

---

48 Both onboarding graphics were designed by me. I'm such an artist!

When you structure your sales onboarding in this way, you maximize your salesperson's ability to remember the materials, in the context of when they need it, thereby reducing their ramp time and getting them productive and happy!

· · · · · · · · ●●● ● ●●● · · · · · · ·

Onboarding is one of those areas that can be made much more efficient by leveraging a tool to assist with the process. Given my background in marketing automation, I like to think of sales onboarding like a marketing nurture program: You set up a series of informational "drips" in a timed manner, to deliver the information they need at the appropriate stage of a new hire's journey. If the new hire is super-keen, they can choose to accelerate through the journey.

When I was at Eloqua, I leveraged our marketing automation platform to build a new sales-hire onboarding program. This program sent the new hire information they needed, when they needed it. When they clicked through and acted on the emails that were being sent to them, I was able to track them automatically and accelerate the process if they were super-keen. I was also able to duplicate the program and modify it for other sales roles: Sales Development Reps, Sales Engineers, Customer Success . . . the onboarding process was the same, just the content changed.

If I were to build the program now, I would leverage a sales enablement platform like LevelJump[49] to run my onboarding. It's like marketing automation for Sales Enablement – I can build the onboarding program the same as I did so many years ago at Eloqua; but with the added bonus of tracking performance in the CRM system. Which allows me to see how the new hires are tracking against their

---

[49]   Their website: https://www.leveljump.io/

performance and ramp goals, and not just track their content and training consumption.

You need content in onboarding. For your content, you can package the learning materials up in consumable chunks; such as videos or learning guides. All those executives that want to talk at the sales team? Make them record a succinct video so the new hires can watch them at their own pace and instead focus on getting coached on their selling activities.

In addition to boot camps, I have a disdain for quizzing sales reps. Quizzes are dumb.[50] Your piano teacher isn't going to whip out a quiz and test you on your scales, are they? The way to test if a rep has retained the information learned is for them to be observed practicing the selling motion – just like your piano teacher would coach you while you practiced playing. I feel that quizzes are such an archaic way of testing knowledge in sales reps, created only for Enablement to track against their targets instead of the rep's targets. The success of your sales onboarding program should be directly tied to the sales rep's ability to achieve a series of ramping targets. Things like:

- Amount of pipeline created in a set period.
- Number of contacts connected to a new opportunity.
- Time to first or second deal, etc.

Getting your new sales reps onboarded is different than other roles; it's not just about knowledge, it's also about their ability to get into a groove with their process, selling motions and behaviors.

• • • • • • • • • ● • • • • • • • • • •

---

[50]   Yes, that's a *Brooklyn Nine-Nine* reference.

Chapter Eight - Final Thoughts

Your new sales rep onboarding should have a balance of learning information, practicing their daily activities and observed coaching. It should be delivered to them on a need-to-know-basis, so they can put the knowledge into the context of their role. Instead of acquiescing to the will of the executives who want to talk at the new sales hires, insist that they record themselves instead, so you can incorporate those VIP videos into an automated onboarding process that tracks sales performance metrics.

CHAPTER NINE

WHAT DO I DO WITH THE SALESPEOPLE I HAVE?

I don't do sports, but my husband does, and one of his favorite sports to play/watch is tennis.[51] As such, I know who Serena Williams is and I know she is hands-down the greatest tennis player of all time. She didn't get to be the greatest by doing the same thing year after year.

---

[51] The other sport is Formula1, who is a demanding mistress.

She got to be the greatest by working hard with her trainer, watching matches and adjusting her tactics over the years.[52]

The assumption in a lot of sales organizations is if you have onboarded your sales team effectively and they're doing well, then they just want to be left alone to sell. And a lot of tenured salespeople will tell you they don't need training, they just want to be left alone to sell.

Having a structured ongoing Sales Enablement process for your organization is about making certain that those muscles that were developed during the onboarding process stay firm and limber as the salesperson develops in their tenure at your organization. Ongoing Enablement allows them to grow and expand their knowledge and skills, so they don't get stagnant in their abilities. It is there for the sales team to keep in touch with any changes in what they are selling, to whom they sell and how they sell.

I worked with one client who had no structure for the ongoing enablement of their sales or customer success organizations. As an example, if a new product feature was released, there was no formalized process to educate the teams on why that feature should be sold and how it benefited the target customer. As a result, the sales reps would sell on old functionality instead of leveraging common and consistent business use cases on why buyers should care about this new feature. Their Solutions Architects got involved way too early in the sales cycle (sometimes as early as initial discovery) to sell on technical features instead of the rep positioning the deal on the business value of the platform. This created communication gaps, an inefficient sales process and smaller deal sizes.

---

[52] *Fitness Magazine*'s interview with Serena Williams: https://www.fitness-magazine.com/mind-body/inspiration/serena-williams-interview/

An ongoing enablement program should have supporting content and training on existing products, tools and processes, divided into the three major categories I've mentioned earlier in this book:

- **Knowledge.** The products and/or services a salesperson can sell; i.e., what is "on the truck."
- **Sales Skills.** Skill areas that are a challenge for the sales reps; i.e., negotiating, presentation skills, demand generation, tonality, storytelling, etc.
- **Tools/Behaviors.** Ensuring that the teams are leveraging the available tools, process and resources in the right way to close business and create an exceptional customer experience.

An ongoing enablement program can also include:

- Centralized content, information and training for reps to easily access and consume, in one platform.
- Go-to-market content and training on new products/ services and new releases, so Sales understands what they are selling and how it brings value to the target customer persona.
- Content and training on any changes made to target customer persona.
- Sales skills development based on required competencies.
- Career path required training and Key Performance Indicators (KPI) from current role to other available roles (example: CSM to AE).
- Coaching and feedback to sales reps.
- Certification on knowledge, to maintain a consistent message across all sales roles. An example of a Certification

Scorecard to test a sales rep's ability to execute a Sales Play, is provided below.[53]

◢ Sales Play Scorecard
Sales Stage 1

Sales Team Member: **Evaluator:**

_____   _____

Evaluation Approach

The evaluation is scored on a relative ranking with the following scale:

3	Outstanding	Highly prepared with excellent performance of the role-play skill/content being evaluated. Advanced the selling process significantly.
2	Meets Requirements	Well-prepared and good performance of the role-play skill/content being evaluated. **Did everything correctly.** Selling process on course.
1	Needs Improvement	Lack of preparation or awkwardness in execution of the skill/content being evaluated.

A total score of <u>20 or higher</u> is passing for the certification role-play.

Evaluation Elements

	DESCRIPTION	SCORE		
		1	2	3
1.	Opening (*clarify, reasonably pulled the client into the context of the call quickly*)			
2.	Questioning Techniques (*open and closed questions*)			
3.	Listening Skills (*follow-on questions*)			
4.	Summary Techniques (*agreement and confirmation*)			
5.	Plan of Best Next Actions (*what, who, when*)			
6.	Uncovered relevant projects for this year			
7.	Defined success criteria for the project(s)			
8.	Confirmed a demonstration presentation			
9.	Identified the ultimate decision-maker(s)			
10.	Execution of the Sales Play			
	TOTAL			

You can create certifications for anything that requires consistency across your Sales organization, for example:

- Your elevator pitch.
- Your sales presentation.
- A high-level demonstration[54]
- Etc.

---

[53]   I've got lots of these templates, provided as part of my services.

[54]   I call this the "drive-by" demo.

Depending on your organization, you may choose to call the certifications something different; say, "practice sessions" or "role-plays," and you may choose to be draconian or lenient with the scoring. The intent is to make sure that all your revenue-generating roles are consistently delivering the same message.

Once you've established a plan for what your ongoing enablement should entail, you need to set a schedule. The last thing that you need is to create more random acts of Sales Enablement every time something changes! What I have found works well is setting a monthly, quarterly and yearly cadence of enablement:

- Monthly: 45 minutes on the same day of every month to cover quick enablement items, department updates, tips & tricks, etc.
- Quarterly: Larger format enablement, focused on a key piece of knowledge or skill to develop for the team.
- Yearly: Typically, a Sales Kick Off.[55] Cover the meaty enablement items here to start the year off with lots of energy.

This meeting cadence is plenty frequent. If it can't fit into this cadence then it's not important enough to get into the hands and brains of Sales. There are exceptions: If it's something urgent, say, an acquisition or a product failure, then by all means communicate outside of the cadence. Otherwise, if it don't fit, you can't transmit.[56]

• • • • • • • • • ● • • • • • • • • • •

---

[55]   More on Sales Kick Offs in Chapter Thirteen!

[56]   For those of you too young to remember that reference: https://www.youtube.com/watch?v=P_apIbmsUwU

Partners, Channels and Enablement – oh my! Quite often, partner enablement is an afterthought at organizations, particularly if the organization is just figuring out its partner/channel strategy.

If you have a partner/channel strategy, it probably looks something like this:

1. We have partners that need to implement our solution.
2. We have partners that independently sell our solution without us.
3. We have partners that identify where our joint solution could be used, and when they do identify an opportunity, we co-sell with them.

In the case of 1, the folks in your organization who are responsible for implementing your solution are best suited to coaching your partners. You will want to put your implementation partners through the same training and certification processes that are experienced by your internal Services folks.

In the case of points 2 and 3, you have partners who are selling in some degree on behalf of your brand. Which means you should provide them with the same enablement you are providing to your direct sellers:

- What you are selling,
- To whom you are selling, and,
- How to sell it.

I'm going to repeat that: Provide them with the _same enablement_. A lot of organizations struggle with this concept in philosophy, execution or both. Think about your organization and ask yourself this: Are you treating your partners like they are members of the family, or like unwanted guests at Thanksgiving?

What and To Whom the partners are selling are the same as your direct organization. Which means they need the same materials and training your direct organization receives. The How may be different, depending on how the partners engage with your organization to sell your stuff; i.e., do they have access to a partner portal, can they access your internal systems, do they have to co-sell with you, etc.

The bottom line: You need to treat your partners/channel as though they are an extension of your direct salesforce; because everyone who interfaces with your potential customers must deliver a consistent experience.[57]

• • • • • • • • ● ● • • • • • • • •

Chapter Nine – Final Thoughts

Ongoing enablement for your current roles is as critical to your organization as keeping a consistent training and diet regimen is to maintain a high-performing athlete. Set a schedule for when you intend to run enablement for the year, then determine the key pieces of knowledge, skills and behaviors to slot into the schedule. Leave some wiggle room for things that pop up, as your ongoing enablement should be as flexible and iterative as any workout schedule.

---

[57] More on the importance of a consistent customer experience later in this book!

CHAPTER TEN

GET THE RIGHT SALESPEOPLE ON THE BUS

Sales managers think they are fantastic at hiring salespeople. I had one manager tell me, "All I need to do is have a ten-minute conversation with the candidate and I'll know if they are someone I can have a beer with."[58]

Recruiting is one of those areas that is often overlooked at an organization, because HR tends to leave the interviewing to the sales managers and salespeople are fantastic at interviewing. Just because you "could have a beer" with that rep does not mean they will fit into your sales organization. In fact, it's a terrible way to base your interview because – SPOILER ALERT – salespeople are ALL people with whom you can have a beer. That's kinda their schtick: generally outgoing, extroverted, fun-loving, booze-swilling chatterboxes.[59] Salespeople interview exceptionally well, because

---

[58]   His grammar, not mine.

[59]   That is not to say that ALL salespeople are like this; but it's a pretty good bet that the loudest group of people at a bar have some salespeople in it.

their job is to build rapport quickly and develop a relationship that makes you want to buy from them.[60]

Instead of interviewing your candidates on cultural fit ("can I have a beer with them?"), interview them on sales process fit; because what makes a sales rep successful at one company may not necessarily work at your company.

As an example: I worked at a smallish SaaS organization (~400 employees) that got acquired by a huge software/hardware corporation (~100k employees). The sales processes we had at the small organization were dramatically different than at the corporation acquiring us. The salespeople we had that were consistently successful at the smaller company couldn't close business at the larger corporation. The sales people had not changed; they were still the same successful sales reps selling the same SaaS platform. What had changed was the process to manage a deal; more paperwork, less flexibility, different systems. They needed to spend more time on structured selling procedures and did not have the agility they once had at the smaller organization. These new sales processes did not fit with the way these reps naturally worked on their deals; consequently, they could no longer be successful and had to find organizations that had sales processes that were more conducive to the way they managed their book of business.

Enablement can play a role in determining what a good sales rep looks like in your organization and make certain you are hiring for that profile and process. Have a standard set of questions that tests for both process and cultural fit, train the hiring managers on how to ask those questions, and make sure everyone doing the interviewing is in agreement on what you are benchmarking against at the organization.

---

[60]   Or in the case of an interview, buy them.

What I'm going to say next may sound crazy; but TELL the candidate how a salesperson is expected to run their business at your organization. Let them know exactly what they are getting in to, and to what they will be held accountable. The recruiting process is as much about the candidate figuring out if you are the correct fit for them as it is about you assessing their fit . . . don't be shady about the crazy sales processes you have (or don't have). The last thing either of you want is to have a bad fit. The more forthcoming you are with the candidate in the interview process, the more likely you are to get the candidate that is right for your organization.

· · · · · · ● ● ● ● ● ● ● ● ● ● · · · · ·

When I was at that smaller SaaS organization (pre-acquisition), one of the things we used to do to determine if we were hiring the right fit for our sales organization was to have them deliver our sales presentation back to us as part of a second interview, once they had gone through the initial recruiter screening and the first set of interviews. We would provide them with the script for our sales overview presentation and give them every opportunity to ask questions before they came in for the interview presentations. This allowed us to:

- See the presentation style of the candidate.
- Determine if the sales rep was inquisitive enough to ask for guidance prior to the presentation, which was a critical sales skill that our successful reps exhibited.
- See how the candidate made the presentation their own because they were excited about joining our organization.
- Show the candidate the type of organization we were, so they could determine if we were the right fit for them.

This presentation step was hands-down the best way to determine the right fit for our organization because it represented our selling process so well. For your organizations it may be a mock demonstration, or a negotiation call or something else; whatever it is, Enablement can work with your recruiting team to fit it into the hiring process.

• • • • • • • • • ● ● • • • • • • • • • •

Chapter Ten – Final Thoughts

Hiring the wrong salesperson is a costly and frustrating endeavor for both the candidate and the organization. Take your time to assess the candidate's process fit as much as cultural fit, so both parties understand what it means to be successful at your organization.

CHAPTER ELEVEN

HOW DO WE SOLVE A PROBLEM LIKE THE SDR?

It's a sunny Tuesday morning, and you're at your desk, snuggling into your second cup of coffee as you respond to various emails. Your phone rings, and without looking at the call display you answer; because talking to someone on the phone is WAY better than responding to a chain of emails, right?

The person on the other end of the line introduces her/himself, and then launches into a sales pitch on why you desperately need their software. Outside, clouds are rolling in to block the sun. You hear, "Can I book you on a thirty-minute call with my account executive?" What do you say?

If you are like me, you probably say something to the effect of, "We're okay right now, thanks." and then pleasantly say goodbye to the caller, hoping they'll never bother you again. What you don't know is the caller did have a solution that could solve a current problem you actually have.

I have seen many LinkedIn posts disparaging Sales Development Reps (often called BDRs or SDRs) for a "bad call" and "wasting their time." Maybe I'm getting soft in my old age, but the SDR really isn't to blame – it's their organization's sales process and/or enablement.

I was running a training session at a client recently and got into an interesting discussion with an SDR. Here is how the conversation went:

> **Me:** As sellers, we need to always keep the customer at the center of the dialog. It's about them, not about you.
> **SDR:** But, in that initial call, I have a set of discovery questions I need to get through.
> **Me:** And?
> **SDR:** How am I supposed to get through them all, and still tell a story to the customer? I need to know whether to qualify them in as an opportunity or qualify them out and move on!
> **Me:** Say I'm the customer and you call me. If you start asking me a thousand questions to qualify me in, what motivation do I have to answer you truthfully, if at all?
> **SDR:** But that's how I'm measured?

The SDR is typically paid on booking that thirty-minute meeting between you and their sales rep. Their compensation plan is designed to pique your interest enough to take a call with a more experienced sales representative, who will also spend what you may feel is an eternity being bombarded with the same questions designed to "qualify you." The irony is: THEY called you. And yet, they are now qualifying you against a set of criteria designed to determine if you are worthy of a salesperson's time. Suddenly what should have been a call about you is now a call about the sales rep and their product.

If I'm measured a certain way, I'm motivated to reach that goal. Compensation ALWAYS drives behavior. I'm going to repeat that, this time in capital letters because so many organizations fail to realize it: COMPENSATION ALWAYS DRIVES BEHAVIOR!!!!![61] In Sales, my ability to hit my target means I make lots of money and go to President's Club. Conversely, my inability to hit my target means no commission, no money and I end up living in a van down by the river.[62]

The software being sold may be the best thing since bunny-butt doughnuts[63] but the organization is compensating the sales team on a set of internal, archaic markers and not on where the customer is at in their journey. And that SDR is probably one or two years out of school and has never sold anything before; their organization

---

[61]   And with five exclamation points, because why is this so hard to understand for organizations?

[62]   One of the funniest Chris Farley characters of ALL TIME: https://www.youtube.com/watch?v=qFbvwVfWFpE.

[63]   These are the best doughnuts ever invented, and I curse Krispy Kreme for removing them from their spring release. If you've never had one: imagine a cream-filled glazed doughnut, with white frosting, in the shape of a bunny's behind, complete with candy back paws and candy cottontail. Biting into a bunny's butt is the best feeling in the world and I won't apologize for enjoying it!!!

probably hasn't enabled them with the tools and training they need to be successful.

If you compensate SDRs on the sales process, you're doing a disservice to the value of the solution you provide. The purpose of an SDR is to develop sales. The way you develop sales is to get prospective buyers interested in buying your product/service. A buyer won't be interested in buying anything if the first thing they hear is a series of questions designed to determine if they are a qualified buyer. They also won't buy if the second thing they hear is a pitch on how great the company the caller works for is and how the product is saving billions for others.

What the buyer cares about is how their peers are doing things better than they are, and if they stay where they are at, they could fall behind. The buyer wants to know that their world could change for the better by doing something differently than they are now, and how easy it will be to get to that ideal state. Most sales organizations, however, are not empowering their SDRs to have those conversations with the buyer; instead they are compensating the SDR to have a quick conversation and check a status box in the CRM.

I would love to see SDRs compensated on quality of conversations and trained appropriately to get there. Enablement can lead the charge in making this happen.

• • • • • • • • ● • • • • • • • • • •

Part of the SDR problem is companies hire young, inexperienced candidates into the SDR role and expect them to carry on a meaningful conversation with a C-level executive for tuppence a bag.[64]

---

[64]   Now this song will be in my head ALL. DAY: https://www.youtube.com/watch?v=XHrRxQVUFN4.

If you insist on hiring straight out of school for the SDR function, you need to acknowledge that those kids probably have very little to no sales experience. Which means the things you take for granted: writing a professional email, having a succinct phone conversation, office etiquette, etc., are completely foreign to them.

One of the first things I did when designing a new hire program for the SDR function at a large corporation – we hired five hundred new graduates straight from college into the SDR function – was to create and curate basic training courses around the soft skills of sales.

My favorite soft skill? Whiteboarding. The ability for an SDR (or any person, really) to be able to articulate what they have to say using a simple pen and paper drawing is one of the most valuable skills anyone can have. It immediately engages the other person, establishes credibility for the SDR and forces the SDR to really know what they are talking about. When you sit next to someone at a conference and can sketch your solution out on their cocktail napkin, it creates a human connection that is more impactful than any PowerPoint pitch.

My second favorite soft skill? Storytelling. I love a good story . . . every human does! No one wants to hear a sales pitch, but everyone will listen to a good story, especially if it's about themselves. And even better if it's structured like a movie – because who wouldn't want to watch/listen to a movie about themselves!

Most movies follow a very specific structure[65] about transformation. In this case, the movie is about the target customer's transformation from where they are now to using you. Your elevator pitch should sound

---

[65]   Read **Save the Cat** by Blake Snyder if you'd like to learn more: https://www.amazon.com/Save-Last-Book-Screenwriting-Youll/dp/1932907009. Reading is fundamental, children!

like the logline of your sales movie, to entice the listener into learning more. Your sales movie should flow something like this:

- The customer is in a current state. But then something happens (a catalyst) that sends them on a journey of transformation.
- You are there to guide them on that journey, not swoop in to save the day. You are not Mighty Mouse.[66]
- The customer will go through some peril if they don't complete their transformation.
- The customer's final state is using you to achieve their dreams, completing their transformation.
- The customer lives happily ever after, as they are getting value and looking like a rock star, using you.

If you arm your SDRs with the ability to tell a compelling story about the customer, it will create a great experience that sets you apart from all the other SDRs calling into that customer.

And my third favorite soft skill? Improv. I've already covered my thoughts on improv in Chapter Five, and improv is an especially important skill for young sales professionals who really need to know how to adjust and pivot in a conversation based on what the prospect is telling them. You can't teach fifteen years of selling experience to an SDR; but you can teach them how to listen and improvise so they sound like they have fifteen years of experience.

• • • • • • • ● • • • • • • • • •

It amazes me how many organizations do not provide a documented career path for their employees. It's as though we've all just accepted

---

[66] For those of you too young to remember: https://en.wikipedia.org/wiki/ Mighty_Mouse

that employees won't be around in their roles long enough to need to know where they are headed in two to five years at the organization.

You must provide a development path for sellers. Particularly for the younger salespeople, who may be starting out in an SDR role and are eager to become quota-carrying after a year.

Yes, I said a year. *grumble* these kids today with their loud music *grumble* . . .

For many people, one year in a role is as long as it takes to become partially proficient; yet, there is a desire amongst younger generations to get to the perceived next level in their career after a certain time. I have worked with new SDRs out of college who believed that after one year as an SDR – regardless of how successful they were – they should be promoted to a quota-carrying rep. Hey, if someone is crushing it as an SDR and turning that rep into an SDR after six months makes sense, then by all means, but time spent in a role should not be the only deciding factor.

Even your most eager SDR cannot argue with a defined sales role path, one that measures sales skill level, goal achievement, behaviors, and time in a role. And why not make it a visual career path for the SDR, so they know exactly what it takes to get to the next sales role level? Just like this one from SalesLoft[67]:

---

[67]   Original article from SalesLoft here: https://salesloft.com/resources/blog/career-progression-sales-development-rep/

This example has a combination of goal attainment, measured achievements, and time in the role. It's a clear definition of the path to get a promotion, and it gives a young SDR guidelines on how to get there. There is no ambiguity about what is expected and the behavior it will take to get there. It's up to them how much they want it!

Providing clear, visual career paths for your sales roles will go a long way in fostering behaviors of growth and collaboration.

I should note that not every SDR is destined for a quota-carrying sales role, but that does not mean you should remove them from your organization. Some of the best Sales Enablement professionals I have worked with started out as SDRs, then realized they just weren't interested in the intensity of closing deals. These were SDRs who were willing to coach others on their best pitches, the SDRs who had the best hand-off calls, the SDRs who had the fastest "sales hacks" they used to manage their day . . . all things that make a great Enabler! So, if you are looking to hire someone for Enablement, look at your SDR team and see if there is anyone you can guide on a career path of taking what they know about the sales process and funneling it into enablement activities.

* * * * * * * * ● * * * * * * * * *

Social selling is such a hot topic, and many organizations struggle with this sales tactic. I, on the other hand, struggle with accepting "social selling" as a new concept. From my perspective, selling has always been social! Sales professionals have been engaging with their buyers for years – it's the medium that sales reps now use to connect with buyers that has transformed.

Eighteen years ago, when sales reps wanted to reach out to potential buyers, they would pick up the phone and call them directly. Other than calls, direct mail and in-person meetings were essentially the only ways to make connections. But the world rapidly changed and there are so many new ways the buyer can circumvent the sales rep to get relevant information during the decision-making process.

Guided by this new truth, your sales organization should consider developing a multi-channel engagement approach for all sales interactions; ESPECIALLY FOR YOUR SDRs. It's not just about building a relationship, but also consideration for where the foundation of the relationship is built. Here are three ways you can enable your SDRs in the social theater:

Elevate your SDRs' profiles

Start by training your reps to leverage LinkedIn to build their professional brand. Teach them to focus on emphasizing instances where they provided value to clients rather than simply listing their professional accomplishments. In other words, work with your SDRs to develop professional human profiles, uniquely branded around what makes them special. If a buyer was to do a web search on your rep, they'd find a LinkedIn profile that established the rep as a valuable resource with which to engage, and maybe even someone they'd like to get to know!

Arm the SDR with insights

Now that your reps are armed with a killer profile, it's time to figure out an engagement strategy. After all, a key part of sales is building relationships on platforms where the buyer is regularly interacting. Some questions you should ask are, "What value can our sellers bring to the marketplace?", "What insights can they provide?" and "Where can they communicate those insights so a buyer would hear them?" You need to understand why a potential buyer would want to connect with your seller. Your reps should spend some time each day consuming content generated not only by your organization, but content related to their industry expertise, the companies they are pursuing, and general topics of interest that will build their professional brand.

Tapping into the power of referrals

With your new engagement strategy in place, it's time to accelerate it. Take advantage of the power of the referral, leveraging individuals within your organization to facilitate introductions and conversations between your SDRs and customers. Prospective customers are more likely to respond through an introduction from a mutual connection instead of a generic, non-personalized connection request.

Adopting any sales process change is a journey, but in today's internet age, it's a mandatory requirement. It allows your SDRs to make warm connections with potential buyers by engaging in relevant conversations. And most importantly, they're building their professional brand and credibility in the space.

• • • • • • • • ● ● ● ● ● ● • • • •

Chapter Eleven – Final Thoughts

Please stop treating your SDRs as a task-driven function and use them instead as your first point of engagement in creating an exceptional customer experience. When organizations shift away from sales process-centric production line selling and embrace a more customer-centric approach to calling and compensation, it will set those organizations apart in this age of the internet.

CHAPTER TWELVE

SALES MANAGER? I DON'T EVEN KNOW HER!

There are two big mistakes I see companies make when it comes to setting up the function of Enablement:

1. Assuming their sales managers know how to manage salespeople.
2. Assuming their sales managers are on the same page when it comes to enabling their salespeople.

A large percentage of sales managers were once quota-carrying sales reps; in fact, many sales managers have both a team to manage AND an individual quota to carry. Remember how compensation drives behavior? If I can make more money driving my individual commission than coaching a team of folks, you'd better believe most of my time will be spent closing deals. It's unfortunately the reality of sales behavior.

The first recommendation I make to any organization that has these "player-coach" type models for their sales managers is to drop the "player" piece. If the sales manager knows that they are getting compensated on managing a team ONLY, that is where their focus will be.

SiriusDecisions says the ideal delineation of a sales manager's responsibilities is as follows:[68]

The Role of the First-Line Sales Manager

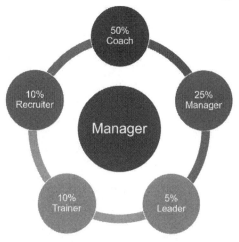

---

[68] Read the blog post here: https://www.siriusdecisions.com/blog/2013-the-year-of-the-firstline-sales-manager.

I remember showing the above chart to a client who exclaimed, "But where is the circle for closing deals with my reps??" The answer is there isn't, because that isn't your job. Let your baby birds fly out of the nest and focus instead on nurturing them in their growth.

Even if your sales managers get the fact that they need to coach their team instead of stepping in to close their deals, there remains the challenge of how they should do it. Most sales managers understand the concept of deal reviews – after all, many of them have gone through them with their own managers at some point when they were individual contributors – but do they really understand HOW to run them?

Your sales managers are the owners of a book of business (for example, a territory or a set of major accounts), and your reps become franchisees of that business. The sales manager then meets regularly to discuss both tactical and strategic aspects of the business:

- On a weekly basis: Meet to discuss specific deals, the immediate forecast and opportunities that are stuck/due to close soon. This is the tactical analysis and should only look ahead to the next couple of weeks.
- On a monthly basis: Meet to discuss pipeline development for the next couple of months. Things like activities to generate demand in their franchise, making sure they have enough opportunities to work on in the quarter to meet their targets, etc. This is NOT the meeting to have deal reviews, as you are already doing that on a weekly basis.
- On a quarterly business: This is the business plan for the rep for their quarter. They should do an analysis of their previous quarter's performance and their plan of attack for the next quarter. This is a strategic review of the rep's franchise. Maybe you discuss a key account to focus on

for the quarter; but this is also not the meeting to do deal reviews.

Here is a more detailed example of this Sales Manager cadence:[69]

The Sales Manager-Led Journey

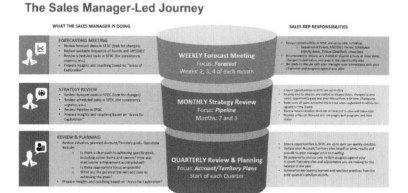

This lists out the sales manager's responsibilities, the salesperson's responsibilities and what is expected during each type of meeting (weekly, monthly, quarterly). By leveraging this cadence, you remove the ambiguity from the manager's responsibilities and give them a framework they can use; so they're not left to their own devices to figure out the whole coaching thing.

• • • • • • • • • ● • • • • • • • • • •

I took an oath when I became an Engineer, vowing to always put 100% of me into my work, because anything less is a blemish on my profession. The reasoning behind this oath is that, as Engineers, we must hold ourselves to a high standard of professional conduct – if we

---

[69]   Another one of my fabulous templates! You get a template . . . and you get a template . . . everybody gets a template!

build something half-assed, it could cost people their lives. Google "engineering disasters" and you'll understand what I mean.[70]

I would prefer to be either ridiculously successful in my career, or crash and burn in a hugely spectacular ball of flame. To me, being mediocre is not an option. This philosophy has always resonated with the Engineer in me, and as such I have adopted a "go big or go home" style in everything I do.

What happens when you realize you are in an organization that is perfectly happy with being mediocre? An organization that is slowly destroying itself through mediocrity? An organization that is the Good Ship Mediocrity?

At first, they may be doing everything you'd expect a company to do in order to effectively pivot: hire the right people and empower them to get the job done, listen to their counsel, adjust quickly and accordingly. You may hear things like, "You're the expert, we hired you to get this done the right way. Get 'er done!"

Music to my ears! A blank canvas to build the perfect system, and the support needed to get it implemented the right way.

Then a key executive departs. And there are only two reasons why executives leave.

1. "I really don't want to leave but I did what I came here to do and now it's time for me to ride into the sunset on my golden horse of stock options."

You can also search for "ritual of the calling of an engineer" if you'd like to read up on the history of the oath.

2. "Imma let you finish, but I completely disagree with everything
    that is happening at the executive level and I'm fed up/being
    asked to leave. So long, suckers."[71]

What happens next can directly impact the course towards/away
from mediocrity in an organization. Either it learns from the executive's
departure and adjusts course . . . or it blames the departed, gets
myopic, and does not see the sharp rocks beneath the surface ahead.

The interesting part about a sinking ship is that unless you hit an
obvious iceberg, it's hard for those at the top to realize their ship is
sinking until it's too late. That's why all the rats leave first – they're at
the bottom of the ship and can see the damage those rocks have
made.

If you're not a rat, and you are not the executive who left, how can
you tell if you're on the Good Ship Mediocrity?

Fortunately for you, Dear Reader, I've been on that ship before, and
will share my findings with you as a cautionary tale.

Warning Sign #1: The culture sucks.

Company culture is so de rigueur. Everyone wants to work for a
company that has a "fun" culture and every executive wants the
business world to know it has a "fun" culture. We have standing
desks! And foosball tables! And snacks in the kitchen! Look at the
social media post of our office doing the *insert the latest social
media challenge*! Aren't we a fun culture!

---

[71]   In case you missed this reference: https://knowyourmeme.com/memes/
kanye-interrupts-imma-let-you-finish

If I see the phrase "Culture eats strategy for breakfast" without any sort of context in a social media post one more time, I'm going to kick a squirrel.[72]

Here is your context: Organizations who truly consider culture a key part of their vision don't just pay it lip service. They live by the core values of its culture. They source those values from its employees. They measure their people by those values; and teams will hold each member accountable to those values.

You can have two, five, seven, ten core values . . . the number is irrelevant. Organizations that have a strong culture (think Disney, Southwest Airlines, Zappos) recruit into the company based on their core values, onboard and train on core values and measure employees on those core values. From interns to executives, everyone not only knows what those values are, they live and breathe them every day.

I was at an organization that kept broadcasting the core values of our culture at every company meeting . . . but no one could ever remember what they were or why they were our core values. Our leader would take every opportunity to spew the core values out to the employees; values that were created in some boardroom with minimal employee input, values that weren't referenced or reinforced by anyone outside of a couple of executives. As the company grew, cliques formed and created silos. Nothing unified the organization. Employees would complain that we didn't have a good company culture and the executives were baffled because we had our core values! We talk about them at every company meeting!

---

[72]   Don't feel sorry for the squirrel. They're furry little bastards who have no regard for you, your garden, or anyone you love.

When people don't understand why they are doing something, they tend to do it half-assed. Not maliciously. They just don't know what full-assed means, because no one understands the why. When employees complain that the company doesn't have a culture, what it really means is they don't know why they are doing what they are doing . . . which means you may be on the Good Ship Mediocrity.

Warning Sign #2: No diversity.

The beauty of bringing a diverse group of individuals together to achieve a common goal is the different perspectives you receive. Those perspectives can help to challenge the status quo and stretch the organization into achieving a level of success that may not have been conceived of if you had a group of like-minded people all parroting the same ideologies. The entire technology industry was founded on "disruptors" – people who thought differently and embraced various perspectives.

You don't go to the gym to eat doughnuts; although, that would be the world's best gym and I would totally go there every day. You go to the gym to be challenged, to push yourself into exercising a bit harder. You know it's working if you are uncomfortable afterwards. Or in excruciating pain that makes you want to vomit. Disruption is uncomfortable. Challenging the status quo is uncomfortable. It's a lot easier to all get along and not rock the boat.

Groupthink is a psychological phenomenon that occurs within a group of people in which the desire for harmony or conformity in the group results in an irrational or dysfunctional decision-making outcome. Group members try to minimize conflict and reach a consensus decision without critical evaluation of alternative viewpoints by actively suppressing dissenting viewpoints, and by isolating themselves from outside influences.[73] I was at an organization that slowly started to replace who they viewed as "disruptors" with people who all got along with each other. People who had the same ideas, who worked together at other companies doing things the same way that they had done them ten years ago. People who didn't like to cause conflict. It was like watching Groupthink in time-lapse. Slowly the office floor became homogenized; no one went to outside conferences, we didn't look to outside sources to validate or benchmark ourselves, and no one read anything outside of what our teams produced.

Warning Sign #3: Blame vs. ownership.

This seems obvious, but it's astounding to me how often this still happens in organizations that employ individuals over twelve years of age. If you're under twelve years old, you get a free pass on this one.[74]

I was sitting across from a head of sales after one of our most successful customer events in the company's history. Any salesperson that had prospective customers attending the event could basically guarantee those folks would become new customers shortly after the event. And when I commented as such to the head of sales, the reply I got was: "Our salespeople aren't very good at closing business. They need more training."

Now as I mentioned earlier, I don't do anything half-assed; I'm either all in or all out. Which means I had built a world-class sales training curriculum, validated by a third-party consulting firm and benchmarked above average against other organizations of our

---

[73] Go read this book on Groupthink, it's fantastic: https://www.amazon.ca/Wiser-Getting-Beyond-Groupthink-Smarter/dp/1422122999.

[74] Also, aren't you a bit young to be reading this book? I'm not judging, just pleasantly surprised.

size. To hear we "needed more sales training" made me want to stab him in the eye with my stiletto.

And yet, because I'm not an inherently violent woman, I evaluated his statement carefully. Was there some truth within it? Was there an opportunity to do better as an organization? I asked, "What is it about the current training they receive that isn't meeting your needs?"

The reply was convoluted and bloated, like most of the statements that came out of this sales leader's mouth. In the interest of saving you from the inanity of what I experienced, it essentially surmounted to the following:

1. He had no idea the extent of the sales enablement curriculum, despite multiple communications on the topic.
2. The training wasn't exactly what his perception of training should be, even though he had never developed sales training in his entire career.
3. It was easier to blame Enablement than to admit he wasn't doing his job effectively.

Assigning blame removes you from the problem . . . but it also removes you from the solution. I have found that it is far more empowering to accept responsibility than to blame others. When you accept responsibility – even when it isn't your fault[75] – you can create a solution that is more beneficial to the company than laying blame ever could.

Now in this case, there was no way I was going to accept responsibility for this not-twelve-year-old-that-was-acting-like-a-twelve-year-old. So I challenged him on his conclusion:

---

[75]   Within reason, of course.

"You understand that sales training is entirely ineffective if the sales managers do not reinforce the behaviors we want to see. Are your people coaching the teams on the skills my team teaches them?"

To which the sales manager on his right said, "Uh, she's right. I don't check to make sure my people are doing anything related to the skills training they receive."

I said, "It sounds like what we actually need to do is put your direct reports through a refresher on how to coach their sales people on the behaviors we expect, so they can put all the great training they get to practical use" while taking a healthy swig of my champagne.

Unfortunately for me, because the company was in a sinking state, I saw the warning signs coming for me shortly after the above exchange. I was removed from the business because I wasn't matching the Groupthink philosophy. Don't shed a tear for me; I was ready and happy for it.

If the leaders in an organization are more willing to blame others than accept responsibility for themselves, then you may be on the Good Ship Mediocrity.

Chapter Twelve – Final Thoughts

If you're going to go down the path of putting in enablement for your customer-facing functions, make sure you enable the managers! Involve them, invite different opinions and revisit regularly so you are never in danger of being mediocre.

We spend so much of our waking hours working for a manager, for a team, for a company, for ourselves. We have one life on this planet.[76] Do you really want to spend that life in a mediocre company, where no one cares if you sink into oblivion?

Allow me to quote Sansa Stark in HBO's *Game of Thrones* when she says to Ramsey Bolton:[77]

> *"Your words will disappear.*
> *Your house will disappear.*
> *Your name will disappear.*
> *All memory of you will disappear."*

Such is the fate of mediocre companies. You should refuse to let that be your fate.

---

[76]   Unless you believe in reincarnation, in which case, you're in the one life that has you currently reading this book, and not the life where you're an Argentinian Jaguar or a garden slug.

[77]   Full clip here: https://www.youtube.com/watch?v=1kDpfcOBNkU

CHAPTER THIRTEEN

SALES KICK OFF OR ON?

How many boring SKOs or sales meetings have you experienced, where all you got out of it was a hangover and some fun times with your colleagues?

I'm someone who loves to throw an epic party. Not Heidi Klum at Hallowe'en epic,[78] but I do spend a great deal of energy making certain that every detail is perfect for my guests.

---

78   Google it.

Before I started producing SKOs, these were the two types of SKOs I had experienced:

1. Everyone got together in a hotel meeting room, with no windows or natural light, and a rotating set of speakers spewed PowerPoint slides at the attendees for three straight days. Maybe you got a fifteen-minute break somewhere; but most likely you squeeze in a session over a working lunch because there is just too much material to cover and some of the presenters went overtime. In the evenings, you got fed some nibbles and you drink to forget most of what happened during the day.

2. Everyone gets sent to a southern destination resort, in Mexico or the Caribbean, and you gather for one hour's worth of "business planning;" then everyone scatters to go snorkeling, hang out on the beach with umbrella drinks and hopefully avoid an international incident.

Organizations spend a considerable sum of money flying everyone to one location to celebrate the new sales year; yet for all the time and expense that is invested in planning the logistics, very little is spent on the quality of the content and interaction of the participants. The top piece of feedback that I hear from SKOs is that participants love spending time networking with other salespeople, yet most SKOs leave that networking to the evening events instead of incorporating it into the actual schedule.

The production of a Sales Kick Off should happen much the same way a party is planned. With over thirty SKOs under my belt, I can safely say I've channeled my inner party planner when it comes to running an SKO. Attendees leave better off than when they arrived and every piece of post-SKO feedback goes into the planning of the next one to make it even more epic.

For those of you about to take on SKO planning, here is some advice to have the event not suck:

- Center the SKO around one key theme. Not some cheesy theme like **Winning!** but something you can rally the entire team around for the rest of the year.[79]
- Maximum time that anyone can speak on a topic without a break or exercise is twenty-five minutes. Seriously, twenty-five minutes. After that time, your audience's retention will plummet exponentially. Break up the speaker's time with exercises that allow the participants to apply what they've just learned to their day-to-day role.
- Plan for at least one thirty-minute break in the morning, one in the afternoon, and give participants a full hour for lunch. Thirty minutes is more than enough time for folks to check email, make a phone call, talk to each other, hit the washroom and grab a coffee/snack. This also limits the stragglers once sessions resume, as everyone has had enough time to handle business.

Perhaps you want to run your SKO remotely, because of the expense of flying everyone to an exotic location. The above rules still apply, you just need to incorporate multiple mediums within your meeting. Things like using the Chat feature, polling, quizzes, breakout rooms and a really fantastic web conferencing platform in order to keep engagement high.

If this still seems like too much for you, I'm a LinkedIn message away.

• • • • • • • • ● • • • • • • • •

---

[79] One year we had a theme called, **Mission: Possible!** which entirely plagiarised the Tom Cruise movie. It was as painfully cheesy as you are currently imagining.

I was working with a client that had over a thousand sales reps worldwide. The Enablement team was responsible for producing the SKO and their leader had her hands full with running all the ongoing Enablement activities at their organization, so she tapped me to deliver an SKO-in-a-Box[80] package to alleviate the stress on her and her team.

Throughout the design process, the Enablement team had an excellent handle on what the sales organization needed for their SKO. They knew the sales skills on which to focus, they knew the tone to set and they all had experience in designing interactive sessions so the sales team wouldn't feel "talked-at" for eight hours a day.

And then everyone else who wasn't in Enablement stepped in to explain what should get put into the SKO. Executives insisted that they each have thirty minutes to an hour to address the sales team. Product insisted that they have ninety minutes to tell the sales team all the great features that were coming up in the year. Marketing insisted that they have ninety minutes to debrief the sales team on the programs that were being run. All departments insisted on thirty minutes to an hour minutes to update the sales team on the latest organizational structure and how it affects them since most of the sales team didn't know who everyone was in their departments.

Despite the best efforts of the Enablement team, politics got in the way, and the bulk of their SKO ended up with a series of talking heads speaking at the sales team. Interestingly enough, the feedback from Sales was that it was the best SKO yet; but I attribute that to the

---

[80]   It's my full-service package that designs and produces your SKO for you. Like a wedding planner, but with less tulle.

organization and resourcefulness of the Enablement team[81] to work with what they had been given.

If you are an Enablement professional that has been in a similar situation, you must ask yourself how much of a career-limiting move would it be to push back on the potential political situation at your organization. I personally don't think any job is worth compromising my quality of work,[82] but you may not have that luxury. Perhaps you can give executives some time in the agenda as a "Fireside Chat", limit it to half an hour, and put it at the end of the day so you can serve BEvERages while they talk. Or ask the product folks if they instead could put what they want to say in a video recording for the sales team, stating that a recording can be used for onboarding new sales reps. There are many ways you can compromise on demands from other departments, while still maintaining the integrity of the SKO schedule you want to deliver to your sales team.

$$\bullet \; \bullet \; \bullet \; \bullet \; \bullet \; \bullet \; \bullet \; \bullet \; \bullet \; \circledbullet \; \bullet \; \bullet \; \bullet \; \bullet \; \bullet \; \bullet \; \bullet$$

What are the key components to a great Sales Kick Off?

Start with a theme. That theme, as I mentioned earlier, should be something that you can refer to and reinforce throughout the year. The best sales organizations I've worked with take the SKO theme and use it in all their training and sales meetings throughout the year; making it a rallying cry for the organization.

Next, determine how long you need SKO to be. My recommendation is no longer than three full days; ideally, you want to be somewhere

---

[81] With my guidance, of course. Even though there were politics involved, I still produce a great event for my clients!

[82] Which is why I now work for NO ONE! Corporate politics makes me itch.

in the two and a half-day mark, as you can use the extra half-day for folks to travel in/out to the SKO location.[83]

Gather your internal stakeholders. Typically, your sales leaders, someone from Marketing, and your Sales Operations and/or Enablement. Beware of too many chefs in the kitchen, as you'll lose control of the agenda quickly. The question I always ask my clients is: What do you want the attendees to FEEL, KNOW and DO by the end of SKO? After brainstorming ideas, your theme will start to surface.

Make sure you've got someone who can run event logistics. This is typically an event marketer, an executive assistant or an office manager. Discuss the budget with this person so you know the dollars you've got at your disposal; the budget can mean the difference between eating steak or hotdogs.

Then get your stakeholders to brainstorm topics that need to get covered to take advantage of the beginning of the sales year. These can range from sales skills training to product information to inspirational topics. The goal is to get as many session topics onto the table so your agenda can start to take shape. YOU ARE NOT DESIGNING SESSIONS AT THIS STAGE! Just get ideas out of everyone's heads first. I've had some clients survey their sales team as well, to get their input on topics they'd like to see covered at SKO.

Once you get all the possible topics listed, you should be able to bucket them into sub-themes. Prioritize those sub-themes to determine what topics stay in the SKO and what topics need to get moved to a subsequent sales meeting or Enablement session. Ask yourself if the topic takes advantage of the attendees in the room or is it a topic better served by a web meeting or recording. The goal in designing

---

[83]   Or use the half-day for team meetings outside of the SKO.

each session is to make it interactive and engaging; no one likes to be talked at for eight hours in a windowless hotel ballroom. Or in the case of remote SKOs, talked at via a web conference platform while you are all on video camera trying to look like you're paying attention.

Now it's time to chart out your day: start time, end time, lunches and breaks. Time is your constant here, and you'll be able to quickly see how many sessions you can realistically fit into one day without making people's heads explode.

Who are your attendees? Is it for Sales only? Sales and Marketing? Sales, Marketing and Customer Success? Everyone at the organization? SKOs are a great excuse for other departments to tag along; be wary of attendees who have no function in a session. I was running an SKO for a client whose HR department sent two attendees, because they were responsible for recruiting sales talent into the organization. They were on their laptops checking emails and doing other work the entire time they were at SKO, not participating in any of the sessions; which is an incredible waste of time and expense for the organization. If you have scope-creep on your attendee list, it can adversely affect the experience attendees have at your SKO and blow out your budget.

Are there things that the attendees need to review in advance, in order to arrive at SKO prepared for the sessions? I am a huge fan of creating what I call a Certify to Fly program for SKO, which essentially requires each attendee to complete a set of pre-work in order to earn their seat at SKO. One organization I worked at even went as far as revoking invitations to those who had not completed their preparation requirements, cancelling their flights and publicly calling them out. Of course, you need to have the ability to measure and track completion if you decide to put in a Certify to Fly requirement; easily done in an LMS or Enablement platform.[84]

Depending on how many attendees you have at SKO, you may want to put an event app in place to communicate the schedule and encourage interaction with the attendees. This allows you to make changes to the schedule and update attendees in real time, without needing to worry about reprinting materials and killing trees.

Finally, expect the unexpected. The schedule should have enough wiggle room to accommodate last-minute requests, changes in structure and speakers going overtime.

· · · · · · · · · · ● ● ● ● ● ● ● · · · · · ·

Chapter Thirteen – Final Thoughts

You are investing a lot of time and money bringing everyone together for a Sales Kick Off; make it count! Whether you plan to run your meeting in-person or remotely, have a good balance of learning, interactivity and fun so the sales team feels it was time well-spent out of the field.

---

[84]   Such as LevelJump, which I've mentioned earlier in the book.

CHAPTER FOURTEEN

NOBODY CARES
ABOUT YOU.

I remember a fabulous vacation my husband and I had with two other couples in Curaçao[85] a few years ago. We all have a great time together, and it was as we expected: beautiful beaches, friendly people, fun times. What I did not expect was to leave with a key insight into the customer experience.

---

[85]   More on this beautiful island here: https://www.curacao.com/en/

At the baggage claim exit of Curaçao airport, holding a sign with our names on it in cheery letters was "Taxi Max," because he drove a taxi and his name was Max. He was the driver for the rental car company we used, hired to take renters from the terminal to the rental office. Max shook each of our hands, learned all our names, and welcomed us to the island. He then proceeded to take three red paper napkins from his pocket, and while asking us questions about what we'd like to get out of our vacation, he made each female in our group a paper napkin rose, with the flourish of an origami ninja. Once the gals had their roses, we hopped into his taxi and were at the rental car office shortly thereafter. In the taxi, he distributed water bottles and candy, all while giving us his take on what to see and do on the island while we were there.

Even though we had just spent the better part of six hours on a plane, then another hour in customs, and we wanted to get the rental cars and get to our destination, my travelling companions and I were not at all annoyed – we found the experience a delightful way to start the holiday.

CUT TO: It's the end of our vacation, and we are returning the cars to the rental agency. This time there was an agent available to drive us back to the airport in their rental agency van. When we arrived at the airport, after unloading our baggage, she smiled, shook all our hands and said, "Please have safe travels home. Thank you for renting your cars with us for your vacation."

That one statement really resonated with me: simple, appreciative, direct. She knew we were focused on getting checked in and home, so she didn't belabor the experience.

Both experiences with this rental car company were delightful. Neither cost the provider money.

Both Taxi Max and the rental car agent were empowered to provide an experience to us. Both understood the stage we were at in our journey and adapted to our needs: Taxi Max knew we were starting a vacation and provided the appropriate amount of welcoming flourish. The rental car agent was polite and efficient, knowing we were occupied with making our way home.

· · · · · · · · ● · · · · · · · · ·

In this age of providing your customers with memorable experiences, are you enabling your people to use their judgement on what is "delightful," based on where the customer is in their journey with you? First, a quick summary of what I mean when I say "customer journey:" a potential customer engages with your company pre-sales in different ways (possibly via various online channels), then they become a prospect and interact with your sales force, and then they become a customer and work with your post-sales organization as they implement the product. Too often, Sales and post-Sales are siloed organizations, and the hand-off between these two functions is clunky, affecting the customer's experience.

Why does creating a unified customer experience matter? If the customer does not feel they are getting a consistent experience when they are engaging with each member of your organization, the customer will start to regret making the purchase. They could potentially not implement your solution, and eventually leave you.

You want to maintain this holistic customer experience from the point in time when they engage with your brand right through to potentially creating a customer for life. In order to do that, you need to make sure that every role interacting with the customer is saying the same thing and speaking the same language. If your salesperson says one thing and your customer success person says something entirely different, the customer starts to wonder if they are dealing with the same company. There is a dissonance created for the customer, which is bad.[86] Consistency is key to driving a holistic customer experience.

• • • • • • • ● ● ● ● • • • • • • • •

I've focused this book on Sales Enablement, but what about enabling the folks who talk to the customer at every stage of the journey? Lately, the term "Revenue Enablement" is being thrown about by analysts – it's about making certain that everyone from your organization who talks to the customer is saying the right thing at the right time on that customer's journey with you. Successful organizations put several major pillars in place to make customers successful:

1. Have Enablement for all roles in your organization who interact with a customer. In addition to Sales, this means Customer Success, Support, Professional Services, and Marketing.
2. Have a new customer "onboarding" process, so the customer is enabled with what they need, when they need it as they start their journey with you.
3. Have an effective communications process between all departments within your organization that interact with the customer, so everyone knows their roles and responsibilities to the customer at the appropriate stage of their journey with you.

Allow me to expand on each of these pillars.

---

[86]   Why dissonance is bad for your brain: https://www.nature.com/news/why-dissonant-music-strikes-the-wrong-chord-in-the-brain-1.11791

1. Enable all roles

Successful organizations focus on the entire customer lifecycle, and not just on new customer acquisition. Once a customer buys from you, there are whole teams that are responsible for keeping and growing those customers. Whatever you are doing to enable the salespeople responsible for creating new customers, you need to enable the people responsible for keeping and growing those customers. Many of the tenets in this book are applicable to the teams that are charged with keeping and expanding the customer base.

2. New customer onboarding process

As soon as the customer signs on with you, they are in danger of experiencing buyer's remorse. By having a customer onboarding process, you mitigate that danger. Even something as simple as a welcome email thanking them for their business and access to online training they can take as they wait for the next stage in the implementation makes a huge impact on the customer's perception and comfort with their purchasing decision.

3. Cross-department communications

It always amazes me at how siloed organizations are in today's internet age. After a salesperson closes an opportunity, it goes to an implementation person . . . and the customer must go through a whole new cycle of answering the same questions they answered with the sales rep. It's 2020 people – TALK TO EACH OTHER! Leverage your CRM system to capture customer data, so everyone in the organization has a 360-degree view of the customer. Have regular meetings to discuss customer hand-offs, so the transition from Sales to Customer Success/Services is seamless to the customer. By creating those communications channels between departments, the customer will feel like they made the right decision in choosing you.

• • • • • • • • • ● • • • • • • • • •

There is an alarming statistic out there, courtesy of SiriusDecisions research: 71 per cent of sales leaders say it is the salesperson's inability to articulate value to the customer that separates high performers from low performers. Which means only 29 per cent of sales conversations hold any value to a customer.

Salespeople: Stop boring customers with how long you've been in business. Stop talking about all your nifty features. Stop talking about your awards. Because YOUR CUSTOMERS DON'T CARE ABOUT YOU!

The ways customers interact with brands has changed dramatically over the last ten years. Communities, forums and advocacy-as-a-service (the customer experience equivalent of software-as-a-service) options are gaining ground. As a sales professional, if you aren't helping customers understand how and where they can engage with your brand and with other customers, you're just another self-centered vendor trying to sell what's in your trench coat.[87] Salespeople need to be out among customers, encouraging community participation, sharing insight and learning what holds value to the customer base.

It's so critical to break down silos in your organization and spend time with your customer success/services/support teams. They're a fantastic group of people who love your customers, and they have fascinating insight into how your customers gain value from leveraging your platform.

---

[87]   Although I would totally buy an 8 from this guy: https://www.youtube.com/watch?v=rfelvl_ikf4.

What kind of impact can a bad experience have on a customer? Well, do you remember that scene in **Pretty Woman**, when Julia Roberts' character is treated poorly when she enters a luxury store?

At around 6:15pm on a weekday evening, a call came in on my cell phone. I could see from the call display that it was my bank. Typically my bank calls if there is a question about our accounts or credit card, so I picked up the call with a, "This is Melissa."

The response was, "Hello, this is Your Bank[88] calling. Is Mr. Melissa's Hubbie[89] there?"

My husband and I share our bank accounts. I asked, "Is this an urgent matter regarding OUR bank accounts?"

The response was, "No, not urgent, we'd just like to speak to him regarding his accounts."

At this point, I'm annoyed for multiple reasons:

1. I have been a customer of this bank since I was ten years old. I have had these accounts, and have added to them significantly, since that time.
2. My husband could therefore be considered the secondary user on the accounts, as he was added to them when we got married.
3. Since we share these accounts, we have equal say in what happens with them.

So my response was, "He is not available," – actually he was sitting next to me on the couch with a puzzled look on his face as to why

---

[88]   Not the actual name; but I don't need to publicly shame the bank.
[89]   Name hidden to protect the not-so-innocent but very, very shy.

there was smoke rising from my head – "I am his wife, we share our accounts, can I help you with something?"

And the response was, "No, I'll call back another time. Thank you."

I looked at my husband and said, "I'm going to move all our assets away from this bank."

They had one job – ONE JOB – to keep me as a valued customer. And instead, one sales call turned me against them. If you are in Sales, Customer Success, or interface with customers in any way, there are some simple things you can do to avoid making the colossal mistake my bank made with me in that brief phone call.

1. Do your mothertucking[90] research on your customer.

If this sales agent had taken a couple of minutes to LOOK at my account history, they would have seen my longevity with the bank and that I am the one who does most of the transactions. Also, they called MY phone number and not my husband's, both of which are listed on our accounts, which was a dead giveaway that the agent had done NO homework. A little bit of research (in your CRM, online, etc.) will go a long way in creating rapport and credibility with your customer.

2. Listen to the customer!

I gave this agent multiple openings to have a conversation with ME about OUR shared accounts. Instead the agent chose to ignore me in favor of whatever script they were following. If they had just listened, they would have picked up on the fact that they could have the sales conversation with me instead. Whenever you have an

---

[90]   Thank you to RuPaul for this fabulous phrase.

opportunity to get on the phone with your customer, use it to listen to what is important to them so you can adjust your sales/service pitch accordingly.

3. Be present.

Had this agent been present instead of trying to get to whatever objective they had on their call sheet, they may have been able to complete their upsell or whatever objective they had in trying to reach my husband. I see so many sales and customer success folks not be present in the moment they have with their customer, which prevents them from improvising in the moment to ultimately lead to their goal on the call.

How you approach the customer experience can make the difference between creating an angry detractor or building a loyal advocate.

• • • • • • • • ● • • • • • • • • •

Chapter Fourteen – Final Thoughts

Think of your customer experience as a relay race. If the customer is the baton, they start with Marketing, then are passed over to Sales and finally are handed off to Customer Success/Professional Services. Whomever has the baton passes it over to the next role, who then must successfully grab that baton and run with it.

If each member of these functions is not properly enabled they won't be able to run with the baton effectively, or worse, they could drop the baton – which means you lose the race. As an organization, you can't afford to lose any race involving your customers; without them, you do not exist. Always keep your customer at the center of your enablement focus.

CHAPTER FIFTEEN

THAT'S ALL SHE WROTE!

I once moderated a panel of sales & customer success leaders discussing the DNA of a top Sales/Customer Success rep. The topics ranged from what they look for to how they got to where they are in their careers, which got me thinking about my own career. And since we're at the end of my book and I'm in a reflective mood, I figured I'd share my key learnings.

Do more than what you are paid to do. This is the essence of where I am at today. Twenty-five Sales Kick Offs ago I was running a Sales Engineering team when it became obvious that we were in desperate need of someone to run an effective SKO that was more than just awards and cheerleading and boring PowerPoint presentations. It wasn't my job, but it was something the organization needed to be successful. That one task led me to run the Sales Enablement function, where I've been ever since.

Never be afraid to look like an idiot. I can't count the number of times I've said something without thinking, offended someone with my sharp tongue[91], or made a mistake. Every single time, I've owned up to it – because the only thing worse than making a mistake is not accepting that you've made one. Which leads me to . . .

---

91   Probably in this book.

Always be learning. Life is a journey, and every day is an opportunity to learn something new, share in a unique experience, extend your skills. The faster you accept you don't know everything and that you can always learn more, the faster your career will progress.

When I had the opportunity to participate in a course on Leadership Excellence and Employee Engagement at the Disney Institute, I was all over it like Winnie the Pooh on honey. I have no connection or affiliation with the Disney Institute, it's just my opinion that if there is only one course you can pay to send yourself/an employee to, I highly recommend one of the Disney Institute sessions – they are THAT. GOOD.[92]

I learned many valuable lessons from the Disney Institute; one comment from my Disney Institute instructor stood out in particular: "An employee's personal values will always win over the company's values."

Your company's mission may change over time, but your core values are always the same. Use those core values to guide everything: recruiting new hires into your organization, onboarding new hires, ongoing employee engagement, etc. This allows you to align your people with the company's core values; in moments of crisis or stress, you can predict how the organization will react.

Why is it important to have an employee's personal values align with the company's values? If you've read any news of something happening at a company that seemed to be a questionable experience, it's likely a mismatch of personal and corporate values that are the root cause of the issue. Not-so-great things can happen in an organization that has a conflict between the values of the employee and the values of the company. And if you have a company

---

[92]   I get nothing by promoting this; I'm just a fan: https://www.disneyinstitute.com/

culture by default (vs. by design), it's difficult to force alignment with your employees' personal values.

It made me think about my career progression and what prompted each move I made from company to company. Looking back at my career through that lens, it was astonishingly clear: each move was because my personal values did not align with the company's values. And when the company tried to inflict their values on me, it caused a dissonance.[93] That led to my unhappiness and prompted me to look elsewhere, and eventually leave. Conversely, for the company I stayed at for the bulk of my career, my personal values were perfectly aligned with the company's core values, and those values were reinforced in everything we did – hiring, onboarding, coaching and reinforcement. Those values even influenced how we interacted with our prospects and customers; because everyone in the organization lived them every day.

Dear Reader, take an honest look at where you are now in your career progression. Are your personal values in line with your company's core values? Are your team members' values aligned with the company, and with your, values? Can you adjust how you recruit, onboard and coach your people that allows for alignment of those values? I hope you find yourself in a company culture that aligns to what you stand for personally. If not, you may be stranded in a coffee shop of your own, surrounded by disinterested people.

• • • • • • • • ● ⬤ ● • • • • • • • •

Social media is an interesting beast. On the one hand, it's a great way to stay in touch with family, friends and colleagues from around the globe. On the other hand, it's a quagmire of selfies, political opinions

---

[93] Reminder, dissonance is bad: https://www.nature.com/news/why-dissonant-music-strikes-the-wrong-chord-in-the-brain-1.11791

and screaming at each other. My biggest issue with social media is the duplicity it creates within us: for many, the persona posted online is different than the persona at home with people you trust.

I've balked at this idea of duplicity in social media – anyone who has met me or heard me speak knows that the person they see/follow on social is EXACTLY the person I am. And whether you like me or not, at least you know that I'm authentic – with me, you get what you pay for.

I primarily use LinkedIn[94] for the purposes of staying in touch with colleagues and Instagram[95] for staying in touch with family, friends and everyone else. As I was writing this book, I decided to try a little experiment on LinkedIn: crowdsourcing the title of this book. The response was quite overwhelming, although to be fair, I didn't use any of the suggestions provided. Here is a collection of the responses, all excellent ideas:

What I did do was take the advice of the folks who posted and stayed true to who I am and the persona you all see on my social media . . . hence the cheeky title of this book. After all, if I am going to write a book, it should be as authentic as I am on stage, in person and on social.

---

94   Find me on LinkedIn: https://www.linkedin.com/in/melissamadian/
95   Find me on Instagram: https://www.instagram.com/melissamadian/

For those of you who are hesitant to get on social media for the purposes of enablement – I totally get it. It's a cold, often scary place that leaves you open to comments and criticism. On the other hand, like my crowdsourcing experiment, it can reveal some of the best ideas and connect you to people you may not necessarily have the opportunity to meet in person. Start small by posting articles written by your Marketing team, then branch out by posting about neat things you are doing within your organization that can potentially help other folks in your position. You will be surprised at how quickly folks will rally to support you and contribute to the cause of Enablement.

· · · · · · · · ●● ● ●● · · · · · · · ·

In this book, I've covered the basics of Sales Enablement, specifically:

- Sales Enablement is arming your sales force with the knowledge, skills and behaviors they need to be successful in your organization.
- Sellers need to know three key things to be successful:

  o   What they are selling.
  o   To whom they are selling.
  o   How do they sell.

- Hold Sales Enablement accountable to revenue metrics, so you can prove the value of the function to the organization.

If you can master[96] these basics of Sales Enablement, you're well ahead of where most organizations are, and on your way to the next phase of enablement.

---

[96]   I mean "master" in a non-gender specific way; saying "If you can mistress" sounds a little odd.

The next phase is to align your enablement to the Customer's Journey, making sure that all revenue-generating roles have the knowledge, skills and behaviors they need to create a fabulous customer experience that builds customers for life. If you can orient your Enablement around the Customer, then you're a visionary.

At a minimum, as you develop your enablement programs, always put yourself in the head of the customer, and ask yourself: Based on this experience, would I buy from this salesperson?

As for me, it's time to progress to the next stage of my career. In the immortal words of the great goddess Cher: You haven't seen the last of me.[97]

---

[97] So iconic: https://www.youtube.com/watch?v=LD7UtPtyuV8

ABOUT THE AUTHOR

T. Melissa Madian has spent the past twenty-five years in sales, with the mission to make sales and customer success teams more effective at generating revenue while delivering an exceptional customer experience. She is currently the Founder and Chief Fabulous Officer at TMM Enablement Services Inc. She was one of the first people to pioneer the "sales enablement" role within an enterprise corporate structure, and has successfully produced countless Sales Kick Offs, built world-class sales onboarding programs and created enablement structures for many SaaS companies. She is one of the 15 Top Sales Influencers to Follow in 2020, one of the 20 Women Leaders to Watch in Business in 2018 and ranked 10th of the 35+ Most Influential Women Leading B2B Marketing Technology. Melissa loves cats, champagne and her husband (in that order). If you enjoyed this book, she also has a children's book available called *It came from the SCIENCE LAB!!!* and all profits of her children's book go to supporting STEM charities for kids. Follow Melissa on Twitter & Instagram, or connect with her on LinkedIn.

Made in the USA
Columbia, SC
27 January 2022